"THE AWAKING"

STRUGGLING FOR HALF A CENTURY WITH MULTIPLE
MENTAL DISORDERS, NEVER KNOWING WHAT WAS
HAPPENING TO ME, TRYING TO DEAL WITH SEVERE
STRESS AND ANXIETY FROM EVERYDAY LIFE

THEN ONE DAY YOU WAKE UP TO REALIZE THAT FOR
THE PAST TEN YEARS OF YOUR MARRIAGE YOU WERE
JUST A CONVENIENCE,

A MEANS TO AN END, AN ATM MACHINE.
IT'S SURREAL, BEYOND DEPRESSING

I0026742

Dedication

This book is dedicated to my children, which my life would be nothing without them.

Their births are the happiest days of my life. I love them with all my heart and soul. I always have and I always will, no matter what. It's because of them I gained the courage to forge ahead when quitting would have been the easier option. Seeing them every day gave me the courage and drive to succeed.

My fondest memories revolve around the wonderful things they have accomplished and experiences in their lives. I was lucky enough to be a part of. I am so immensely proud of each one of them, and the wonderful adults that they have become.

This book is also dedicated to every person out there that is feeling trapped & alone, struggling with lives little challenges, struggling with a divorce at home. You can do this, you can break free from the lies, the labeling and prejudices society has put on us. Are you ready to make the effort, the rest of your life is waiting for you.

"Don't ever let someone tell you, you can't do something. You got a dream, you got to protect it. When people can't do something themselves, they want to tell you that you can't do it. You want something, go get it. Period."

Will Smith:
The Pursuit of Happiness (2006)

Preface

This story may be hard to believe, I might not have believed it myself if I had not actually lived through it. I can say now that I was able to survive a divorce after thirty-two years of marriage, the last ten years enduring constant, relentless verbal abuse. During most of this time, I was living in a world of confusion. Confused about why I was affected by things in diverse ways than most other people. Constantly having to manage what was an emotional rollercoaster every day. Struggling with mood swings, heightened stress and severe anxiety created a virtual prison in which there was no escaping.

I assumed that this was just my fate in life. It took 50-years for me to get into a position where I was able to realize something could be done to clear the fog. There was a logical reason why my life, my career, and my family were generating such intense emotional feelings. Once the fog lifted, I realized that I was left with a failing marriage. Not wanting to negatively impact our three children I chose to stay in the marriage in hopes that maybe things would get better. Finally, after ten years had passed, I realized there was nothing left, and there hadn't been anything for many years past.

I'm hoping you will be able to learn from my mistakes, you will be able to pick up similar signs in your marriage which may be signaling it may be a time for change. I'm hoping that if you do go through a divorce that it be nothing like the one that I had to endure.

Born in 1962, my parents knew nothing of what a mental disorder was and knew less about how it was affecting their son. I grew up knowing I was somehow different. For decades mental disorders were not acknowledged by the public. How could anyone that was suffering through the challenges these disorders presented have the knowledge of how to deal with these disorders. How could their loved ones know how to cope with these real afflictions? I knew nothing more than to try and deal with my emotions, mood swings and anxiety, as if they were commonplace. However, as we know today, these are quite often too much for any individual to deal with, without professional help. Having a mental disorder is not something that you can just turn off. It took my demeanor to a different level. Looking back, it created difficulties at work and severely impacted my family life and was a contributing factor in having an estranged marriage which ended in a nightmare of a divorce.

I did learn the hard way that there are ONLY losers, and never winners in a divorce. You're kidding yourself if you think that you can come out on top, at the end of all this. There is NEVER a winner, there is only degrees of pain and suffering.

My intent is to help others avoid what battles that they can, while getting through the battles that inevitably have to be fought. I'll share some lessons learned, hopefully this will give you additional confidence that can get you or someone you know through this ordeal without undue stress and depression. There will be a time for a new beginning, putting the pieces of your life back together. The road is going to be filled with obstacles of every kind which will try to derail you, or worse, break you. Rest assured; you must not give up.

For most of you, this is your first divorce. You know little of what is about to be thrust upon you. I know I was clueless. We fantasize that it will be quick, straight forward, with minimal discomfort for you and even your spouse. Knowing full well that the prudent course of action is for neither of you to involve the kids. Who will be adult enough to take the high road, to rise above the temptation using your own children as pawns.

Take a deep look at yourself in the mirror and be truthful in what you see! To what degree would you say you contributed to the events which got you into this divorce situation? It took two of you to make the marriage and it takes two to tear a marriage apart. It will be a challenge for you to rise above any hatred and anger that you may have for your spouse. You must rise above it for the sake and well-being of your children. The number one rule in any divorce that is undisputed by all professionals is to LEAVE THE CHILDREN OUT OF THE DETAILS at all costs.

Plain and simple. If either of you, engage the children in any of the proceedings in the hopes of turning them against the other, you are selfish, callous, and thoughtless, showing no regard to the health and well-being of your children. I can guarantee that later down the road you will regret doing so, and it will haunt you for the rest of your life.

Involving your kids is the largest most impactful thing that you must protect against, but there are many more. The story telling and outright lies your spouse may fabricate to gain favor and sympathy to her false cries of despair will be relentless. There will be controversy, at every turn in the proceedings. I'm telling my story, in the hope that others will be more prepared to survive their own situations.

At this point you may be having feelings that you have somehow failed. Failed your family, failed your marriage, and failed yourself. As a caring parent you should know this not to be true. You provided for your family, if you hadn't provided the best as you could, your family would be worse without all your efforts. It took two people to say "Yes" or "I Do" to start the marriage and it surely didn't fall apart solely because of yourself. If you can look in the mirror and answer the question, did you try to get the marriage to work? Did you try your absolute best to provide and protect for your family? Then you did all you could. Some things are just not in our control.

My goal is to help you put the pieces together, make sense of it all, and move forward with a plan. You need to find yourself, believe in yourself, and never ever give up.

Remember, if you really want something bad enough, then it is worth fighting for!!!

Anything can happen during the divorce proceedings; you must plan for the worst. There is never a winner in a divorce, your goal should be to only survive. Feeling frustrated, lost, or confused, then let's chat; MICHAEL.FUORI@GMAIL.COM

Michael Thomas Fuori
Sandy Hook, Connecticut

What is your deepest fear?

"Our deepest fear is not that we are inadequate. Our deepest fear is that we are powerful beyond measure. It is our light, not our dark that most frightens us. You playing small does not serve the world. There is nothing enlightened about shrinking so that other people don't feel insecure around you.

We are all meant to shine as children do. It's not just in some of us; it's in everyone. And as we let our own lights shine, we unconsciously give other people to do the same. As we are liberated from our own fear, our presence automatically liberates others."

Timo Cruz
Coach Carter (2005)

TABLE OF CONTENTS

Section I: How Did We Get Here

I think people, husbands and wives, mothers and fathers can all agree on one thing; that for there to be a divorce there needed to be a marriage. Two people with common likes, aspirations, become friends, spend time together and have great experiences together. Then as the relationship progresses great friends extend out into great passion between each other.

The two of you are constantly in each other's thoughts. You surprise each other with loving gestures, and thoughtful gifts. You start planning events together, coordinating couples time and me time. Each of you wanting to make the other feel good about themselves, feel important, feel like they belong as a couple. Then, what I feel is the most important of all, is love Every person just wants to be loved and to be able to have someone they can love back.

If this all falls into line, then you have the makings for a great future, and life where dreams can be realized. Quite often though there will be interruptions and complications that will try to derail the relationship. I feel it's kind of a test to see if two people belong together! The ones that will become life partners, ones that can enjoy the good times, and tackle the challenging times, together. It's these types of relationships which are built to stand forever. It's a great feeling when we realize that we have found the one, and they are standing by our side.

A true loving relationship with the one you are going to spend the rest of your life with may just be the first time you have experienced those feelings in your entire life. That does not include your parents. These euphoric feelings bring you into another state of mind. It's like a superpower that you have just discovered you had. It gives you the confidence and the strength to conquer anything life decides to throw at you.

It also makes you do crazy things, like singing or dancing, when you normally do not. In my case I bundled the two. One night my spouse, girlfriend at that time, was in a bar that I owned. It was early and only the workers and some close friends were around. Then of all songs, Super Freak by Rick James was dialed up, and I remember taking her hand and hitting the dance floor, totally out of character for me. It was that feeling that just takes over when you're with the one that you love. Another time, I left the keys at my desk at work, and didn't realize it until closing time. This time my future spouse offered to stay until the morning. My friend parked his car right up against the front door, so no one could get into the bar. The back office didn't have a couch, so there was only one place to sleep, and that was the pool table. This might have ruined the end of a good night for most, for us it was another reason to laugh, it was surely a night to remember.

Another time I will never forget while my ex and I were dating was a time a bunch of coworkers got together outside of the office on a break in the afternoon. It was one of those spontaneous things that just happened. We were all outside and someone knocked my drink off the guardrail, and it poured right into my ex's shoe, which of course she was not wearing at the time. At that time, the only logical thing was to not waste a good drink, so I drank the rest of it directly from her shoe. It made her smile, and I just loved seeing her smile, and I loved the way it made me feel. Everyone deserves that feeling. Her laugh and smile were my kryptonite. It just melted me. It was like a drug that I could never get enough of.

Chapter-I: Family

Life was good, my wife and I bought a house on Long Island, New York. We talked all the time, we loved watching the DIY channel and looked forward to discussions about our future and planning projects together. We loved to dream together.

Then in 1993, before we blinked, our first was born, Austin Michael. Without a doubt the most exciting point in my life. I remember making a video tape of that day, the tape was at least a good solid hour, across the hours leading up to his birth. I was all hyped up on sugar from a duffle bag full of my favorite candy. My ex packed it days before she went into labor. My brother-in-law and I jumped into the car, candy in hand and off we went to make a video log of the day, which I still have to this day.

As parents, we remember how anxious we are in preparing for the moment to arrive, that first breath by your child. Immediately after that would be holding your child for the first time. Words cannot describe these feelings racing through you. You and your spouse created life!

A few seconds after I handed my son back to the nurse, extreme anxiety came rushing over me. For the first time it hit me that I'm going to be responsible for this little baby. How was I going to provide everything for my family over the next two decades. Growing up my dad stressed to me that it was my responsibility to take care of my family, this included making sure my wife never had to work and providing everything they could possibly need. To be honest, it really freaked me out.

The First Sign of Trouble

When my wife and I sat down together to discuss options of her working or staying home to take care of the baby, she was pretty set on staying home, instead of day care. At that point, I was not making much money, barely enough to get the two of us through the month. The benefit is that we agreed that it would be the best thing for the baby. He could be breast fed during those critical years and not have to get exposed to more germs than necessary. Little did I know this decision would slowly drive us apart.

At that point we really could not afford any of the reputable day care centers, so there really weren't any other options that we could afford. However, we did agree at the time, to have her go back to work once the kids got into high school. That never really happened, other than for three years she worked for my consulting company.

Two years later our daughter, Lindsay Genevieve, was born. There was no disputing the job my ex was doing raising our children. I could have never come close to doing the job that she was doing. However, what I started to notice was the way she treated others when it came to raising the kids. Notwithstanding, this included me.

By the time Austin and Lindsay started school, I saw a transformation taking place. My spouse was controlling conversations regarded the kids. It was her way, and no other way. She made everyone very aware that she was in control, and no one would influence "her" kids, period, end of sentence. Even when she and I discussed things in private. She would listen, then conclude with statements like, "that's not going to work," "…. not on my watch," and I loved the short and to the point, "I don't think so"!

Failure is a part of life,
but no one says it has to define you:

"Let me tell you something you already know. The world ain't all sunshine and rainbows. It's a very mean and nasty place, and I don't care how tough you are, it will beat you to your knees and keep you there permanently if you let it. You, me, or nobody is gonna hit as hard as life. But it ain't about how hard you hit. It's about how hard you can get hit and keep moving forward. How much you can take and keep moving forward. That's how winning is done!

Now if you know what you're worth then go out and get what you're worth. But ya gotta be willing to take the hits, and not pointing fingers saying you ain't where you wanna be because of him, or her, or anybody! Cowards do that and that ain't you! You're better than that! I'm always gonna love you no matter what. No matter what happens. You're my son and you're my blood. You're the best thing in my life. But until you start believing in yourself, ya ain't gonna have a life. "

Sylvester Stallone
Rocky Balboa (2006)

Providing For Your Family

In 1995, I started a new job with a software firm, specializing in accounting software. Credit and thanks where credits is due. It was one evening where my ex's brother was talking about his job at diner, and how they were really taking care of their employees along with quarterly bonuses. They were a growing company, so I asked him if he could get me an interview, which he graciously did. After three interviews, I got the job. It involved long hours, and a lot of studying recent technologies, often working eighty plus hours a week. That was the only way to maximize your bonus compensation. Over the next twenty-eight years I made sure I worked as hard as possible, doing whatever it took to provide for my family. Doing whatever it took to become one of the best experts in my field.

What I didn't realize was that as each year passed, my ex's emotional hold over the kids got stronger, and my influence just dwindled away. If I had to do it over again, I would not have worked the hours that I did. At the time I was afraid of being phased out of the project which would have affected my bonus. The family needed that bonus, I couldn't let them down, but at what cost? Missing the kids' events, and everyday moments that make unforgettable memories. I lost out on a lot of great memories because the customer came first. I can't help but wonder if this was the start which led us to living above our means?

If I didn't provide everything that the family requested. If we did not buy so many things, if we stayed the course as my ex and I originally planned, the family would not have gotten into that mindset that dad "loves to work, so why should we get in the way? I would not have had all the stress and anxiety that exponentially grew in me.

As pressures mounted, so did my anxiety levels increase. A big one was when my ex, pressed the "need' to get a bigger house, a much bigger house. Then, came all the furnishings for all the empty rooms we had due to the size of the house. Simultaneously addressing the fixing the house required, and the upgrades which were handed to me. This all drove me to work longer hours and keep ahead of all the innovative technology related to my field. Having the fast paced, self-inflicted, cost of living increases as we were incurring was crazy for me to constantly have to deliver on. I barely had any time to unwind, decompress and relax. It was a never ending battle.

In the case where you are the sole supporter of the family you are taking on a tremendous responsibility. Being the man in the house it's also your responsibility to keep your family safe and secure. The family looks to you to be the pillar of strength.

Living in the northeast, in Connecticut, puts us right in the path of several a Nor'easter which pounds the state every year. Losing power was a common result of the storms. A scary time for little kids. Well, from the day we moved in, it was my job to make sure we never ran out of wood to burn in the fireplace. Sounds trivial, but when you burn as much wood as we did, it was a considerable effort. Many years having to chainsaw, split, stack, and then carry all the wood into the house. With these winter storms often came significant snowfall, along with the countless hours of shoveling and making things safe for walking. Getting over three to four inches of snow would result in an all-day snow cleanup effort. I loved being out in the snow, but it was just another thing that I had to do. This needed to be done within twenty-four hours from the time the snow stopped falling or everything not cleared would turn to sheer ice. The family just expected the snow to clear itself. What was disappointing to me was the fact that most of the time no one would even come out to lend a hand, even after they reached a suitable age to be able to shovel. This is the way it went for decades.

It is not easy to be the sole source of your entire families financial needs. Our society had forced values down our throat that taught us that the man-of-the-house is expected to show little emotions. Newsflash, fathers have emotions just like everyone else, and they can be just as overbearing, as they are for anyone else. Society has deemed it not acceptable to show emotions or talk about our problems openly.

Added Stress & Anxiety

When you find yourself the sole source of income for your family, it immediately puts a lot of strain on you and your marriage. You need to try and find a balance between surviving in your job, trying to work towards advancement, while being available for family gatherings, kid's events, and then an occasional date night and or "quiet" time just between the two of you. All of this can weigh heavily on you. A burden which you should not have to tackle alone.

It becomes stressful trying to manage your schedule. Throw in the challenges of the demands from your day job creates quite the dilemma. It's your job that provides for your family. You must admit your lifestyle as you know it may cease to exist without working hard at your job. Does this automatically put your job at the top of the "Things To-Do" list? What family events does it take precedence over?

Should work always come first? I can now say, unequivocally, no! Work should not come first. Work comes first during work hours, barring any family emergencies. Work cannot rule your life. I know, because from the time I started working, I had my own landscaping business, at the age of fourteen. It was balls to the wall, every day. I only had one speed, to push it as close to the red line, without blowing my engine. Looking back my advice to you is don't let your career define you.

Later in my career I was fortunate to have enough experience and contacts to be able to start my own business. It allowed me to better manage my ADHD and the challenges it posed, specifically the ability to finish what I started. However, the anxiety I now felt was the stress that overcame me in knowing that I was now responsible for finding work for my employees, hence responsible for their family's welfare. This ended up increasing the impact of being bi-polar. The company was successful, but I was always afraid of not being able to produce for everyone. This in the end had me working more hours than ever before. Increasing the stress and challenges on the home front.

The thing about being the sole provider for the family is that you are also taking on all the stress and responsibilities for the family. Quite often the family doesn't see the struggles you must deal with, and they don't understand the stress which comes with trying to provide the family with a certain standard of living. In my case it extended over years, with each year becoming harder than the previously.

My mistake was that I blindly went about doing whatever it took to provide more for the family. What I should have been doing was saving for the future. My family never learned what it was to sacrifice for something they really wanted. It was always provided for them. My spouse forgot what it was like to have to earn for a living, and just came to expect the kind of life that she thought she deserved.

I remember, the year we were trying to buy a house in Connecticut, I billed 3,300 hours to my client, averaging over ten hours, six days a week, for an entire year, not even taking a single day off! That is what it took to produce the required down payment. Of which I suffered physical as well as tremendous mental anxiety. I was afraid of what would happen if I did not do those hours. Would the client find additional resources to make up for my hours? Or would they replace me? These being a few reasons why I continued to push as hard as I did. I was afraid of failing my family, at least this is how I looked at it. However, what I was really doing was spoiling them.

Did this make me a candidate for father of the year? Quite the opposite, during the divorce proceedings they made up stories that all the hours I was working at clients and turned it into me having all sorts of after-hours activities. Come on, how could I make the level of money that I was, providing them the lifestyle that they increasing grew to take for granted with only working from 9-to-5? But they believed their own lies. What I should have done was to save half of all those bonuses, saved for retirement, and forced an adjustment to the family expected lifestyle. I did none of these, and they all cost me dearly.

Parenting is Not Easy

Being a parent means protecting your children. If you are a parent, you can remember all the child proofing you did before you brought your baby home for the very first time. You might have been better off if you bubble wrapped the child, it might have been easier. It's also our job, as parents, to protect them from people that might hurt them, that includes simple things like Uncle John which whenever he saw them liked to pinch their cheeks. Most of the time he would pinch a little too hard. We feel, at least I do, that we need to protect them against things they might experience which could affect them psychologically and emotionally. We explain things to them in terms that they can understand.

Deep down every parent knows that going through emotional difficulties allows our children to grow and experience life for what it is, but in small dosages. Some of us may have had the experience of explaining to a young child, what happened to the goldfish won at the local carnival, that just disappeared, or it might have been a pet turtle that mysteriously vanished. Knowing it was better to tell them a story at their age than to talk about the finality of death. We dodged the bullet, but we also realize that the circumstances and scenarios that will follow our children growing up will only get more complicated that a little goldfish dying.

We also know that there are things that as much as we try, we can't protect our children from. It might be something simple like being in the same room where adults are having an argument or hearing grandpa use a new four-letter word being used as a noun, verb, or final punctuation in a sentence. We just can't be everywhere, all the time; but that is what life's all about. That is how they grow, how they learn to process tough situations. However, it still does not deter us from trying to protect them from the next thing that might spring up on them. That's part of what being a good parent is about.

Then there are days that not even we as parents are ready for. I will never forget the day that I got a phone call from my ex, one winter afternoon. With panic in her voice she told me to get home right away, that something happened to the family dog. The dog was having health issues, suffered frequent seizures. I rushed home as fast as I could, as there was still snow and ice on the roads from the prior day's storm.

The dog, a Husky named Loki, must have had a seizure while outside and fell into the icy water of the pool. I jumped out of my car, into the back yard, where my daughter was crying, pleading to save him. He was not moving. Without a hesitation I dove headfirst into the freezing icy water, shoes, and all. The water was so cold that it was already icing all around Loki. I was smashing the ice with my fists trying to break him loose.

I knew what this dog meant to the entire family, I knew what it meant to my oldest, Austin, as he called him "his little buddy." At this point I told Lindsay to get out of the cold and I would do whatever I could. I did not want her to see this, but I also didn't want her to see me, as I was struggling to get the dog free of the ice and then pulling him out of the water, I was overcome with emotions. Pleading with God to help me save the kid's dog. It was so hard to tread water while trying to pull him out of the ice.

It was too late; I really don't know when Loki took his last breath as I tried to revive him on the patio of the pool. I couldn't let him go, I held him in my arms for the longest time, emotions flowing with no end in sight, and all I could think of is how I was going to break the news to Austin that his "little buddy", had died. It was at least 10-minutes before I could regain my composure. I wrapped him in blankets, drying him off. There was nothing else I could do. It was the worst feeling of my entire life as a parent, as once again the emotions consumed me.

When Austin came home a few hours later, we were there just inside the front door. I had to break it to him that Loki had a seizure and passed away. All he could do was cry out, "no..no..no not my little buddy!" I started hugging him. That did not last for long as he wanted to go out and see him. We took him out so that he could see him. Then he asked me what we should do next.

I told him to go inside, as it was bone chilling cold outside. The real reason is I didn't want him staring at his buddy, his friend. I proceeded to the tool shed, grabbed some left-over plywood, as I only saw it fitting to build Loki a coffin so that we could bury him. For the next hour or so, I lost track of time, I proceeded to make a casket large enough for Loki to fit comfortably in. I brought the casket down to the patio where Loki was wrapped in blankets. I told the kids to gather up his favorite stuffed animals so that he would have them with him in heaven. I wrapped him in such a way that only his head was sticking out of the blankets to make it look like he was only sleeping. I let the kids pet him goodbye, laying down each stuffed animal around him. We all gathered around the casket where I said a little prayer. They were so good, but still visibly upset. I hurt so bad for them.

It was a bitter cold night, below twenty degrees. I then told everyone to go back inside so they wouldn't get cold. I knew it was time to bury him. The casket was approximately 4' x 4' wide x 2' high. It was sometime in February and the ground had been frozen for a few months. It was not going to be easy digging, especially for Connecticut, where there are mostly rocks and limited soil. I found a quite spot in the corner of the back yard, near the state forest. I started to dig. I got nowhere fast as the ground was frozen solid. I couldn't make a dent. I switched from a shovel to a pickax, and finally broke through the frozen top layer.

It was incredibly stressful digging. Every few inches I would hit more rocks, and then more rocks. At one point I hit a boulder size rock which I needed a six-foot steel pry-bar to work it out of the hole. Three hours later, I could no longer feel my fingers, but I finally had a hole large enough to be able to fit the large casket in. I made a mound of dirt over it and surrounded it with a circle of rocks. I saved two bear stuffed animals to put on top of his grave. I went back inside and asked them if they wanted to say any final good-byes. My spouse stayed inside with Tyler as he was young, and it was cold out. Lindsay and Austin came to pray for him. It was so gut-wrenching heartbreaking to know there was nothing I could do to ease their pain.

In the spring I planted flowers around the rocks and would keep it weeded every year. Loki's favorite bears were still at the front of his grave, years later, and remained there until the day the family had to move.

To this day, when I relive this day in my mind, I blame myself, and I become overrun with emotions. I know there was nothing I could have done. But, as the father, I was supposed to protect them from getting hurt like this. The reality is that these things happen, and for some children that have to deal with much more than losing the family pet. I did what I could; comforting them, while reminding them of the good times we all had with Loki. It was a horrible day, one that I will never forget.

Losing the family dog was God's will, it was hard on the entire family. Now think about losing your children. Never being able to see them or speak to them again. Think about how it feels to know that their actions were substantiated by ridiculous stories supported only by unrelated snippets of the facts. It's sad that my ex found the need to use our children to turn against their father. She knew that was one sure fire way of hurting me the most. Something I would have never done to my worst enemy, which includes my spouse.

Conclusion / Lessons Learned

- Whether your marriage is going well, or you have started divorce proceedings, do not ignore the little things. They could be a telling sign of things to come.

- Things change throughout the course of our life, including our marriage. Try and stick to the plan. Don't be lazy and give in to taking the easy way out. Marriage takes work and if your spouse is not willing to put in the time and effort then that should be telling you something right there.

- Just because you and your spouse may be getting a divorce, doesn't mean you are getting a divorce from your children. Your children will need to know now, more than ever how much you love them. Your children will need the comfort that you will be there for them. They need to understand you're not going anywhere. Despite what your spouse might be telling them.

- Whatever you do, do not try to use them as your pawns against your spouse. It's only going to damage the children in more ways than you could ever imagine. It might even damage your relationship you have with them, depending on their ages, and the relationship they have with their mother.

- In a divorce you are no longer working together as a team, your spouse is working with their own agenda, which I'm pretty sure do not align with yours. I mean really, that is what got you to this point. You must work twice as hard for the things that matter to you. Most importantly your children.

Chapter-II: Divorce was Inevitable

Why at the age of sixty, and thirty years of marriage did I no longer want to be married? The answer is simple, I could not see myself continuing to live the rest of my life in the same manner that I had been living for the previous ten years

I was tired of being abused by my wife. I was tired of being ignored by my children. I was tired of working long hours and having little to show for it. I looked into the future and imagined what my life would look like twenty years from now, and I was horrified with what I saw. It was inevitable that we were going to lose our house. I would probably be strangling in debt and having no hope of retirement. It had to stop!

It was also the little things that were piling up against me that were getting too hard to handle. I found myself increasingly ignoring areas of my marriage that most people would take issue with. As the marriage continued, the signs all led in the wrong direction, but for whatever reason, I just chose to tolerate them or maybe it is more accurate to say, I chose to ignore them. There were constant feelings of stress and anxiety, controversy just made things worse. I would rather give in than have another argument. Of course, this was not a good approach to having a happy marriage. In fact, I feel, this is one of the reasons the marriage finally collapsed. In the end all that avoidance ended with a tornado of destruction in its path.

When I was growing up there was always a lot of loud "discussions" between my parents. After years of being surrounded by arguing, not having the arguing made me feel normal for a little while. I had my fill of being around people that argued all the time. It was too much to handle on top of the stress of everyday life.

I could not continue on supporting a family that had little regard for my wellbeing. Too many years passed where they could care less about the sacrifices that I had made for all of them. They had no idea of the stress and anxiety that I was forced to deal with while trying to provide for them, even though they were unrealistic expectations, from all of them.

There were also things that I never really talked to anyone about. At the time I felt that I really didn't have anyone in my life that I felt comfortable sharing the embarrassing details with. I was ashamed of my own marriage, and embarrassed that I would tolerate the kind of neglect and mental abuse that I had to endured for over a decade. Knowing what went down, it would have been better for everyone if we ended the marriage long before we did.

Nobody Wins

Most people do not like a change in their routine. Maybe it is as simple as being forced to change the brand of coffee that you drink every morning, or maybe being told that for your system, coffee doesn't agree with it, and that you need to quit drinking coffee altogether. I would classify this as an inconvenience, a necessary change for the sake of your health.

Now think about it for a few seconds, think about if virtually everything in your life were to change. Most of it that you would be forced into making the change. A change that you totally disagreed with. A change that would put you in a very awkward position. How would you feel then?

Remember we said there is no "winning" a divorce? Even if one person was granted everything and the other person was granted nothing, they are both losers. You can only survive a divorce, and divorce has no favorites, divorce has no sympathy. Divorce often destroys things that we have worked our entire life towards. Divorce damages relationships, in addition to the couple that is getting divorced. Divorce damages the children affected by a divorce of their parents.

You get my drift, that divorce changes people, and most people hate change. It stands to reason that divorce brings out the worst in people. People transform into these monsters determined to destroy the other person. That being the same person that they could not live without when they first got married. They stop seeing each other as people and feel that this somehow justifies being able to inflict as much pain as possible on the person they think is causing all this change to their lives. What they do not realize is that part of the blame, no matter what the particulars of the divorce are, lies with themselves. There is a lower percentage of divorces where one person is to blame for most all of the situation which forced the divorce in the first place.

In the case of my divorce, my spouse did not have to work for the better part of the time from when our first son was born. She was provided a rich lifestyle. I provided for my family in the only way I knew how, and that was to work as hard as I could, while sacrificing whatever was needed to provide that lifestyle. I sacrificed my relationship with most of my childhood friends, as I moved to a bigger house with more land, in Connecticut. I sacrificed my time with my family which was necessary to provide that lifestyle. With all of this, it then stands to reason that my spouse and my children were angry that the lifestyle that I provided was going to drastically change due to this divorce.

Heed my warning that your spouse may take a defensive position, where she will try to keep as many things from changing as possible. In translation this means that she and her lawyers will try and gain as large of settlement as possible to provide her with as much money as possible so that her cozy little life does not have to change. On the flip side, your spouse may take a full-frontal assault on you and your life. Trying to inflict as much pain as possible. Taking away as much as they can from you. Taking you right to the edge of breaking. Do not try and kid yourself, the only reason your spouse and their lawyers will take their foot off your throat is so that you still can generate income to be able to support them.

If your spouse didn't not have to work during the marriage, most likely, they will have to reenter the workforce concluding the divorce. The big house will most likely have to be sold, your spouse will have to start paying for their own health insurance, their own car and the insurance that comes with it. They will have to pay for everything that previously you sacrificed to afford them. Your spouse will want to say to everyone that they did not need you, and that they don't need you now, but isn't it ironic that the alimony that you most likely will have to pay will do these very same things for them. You can look at it like you are still providing most of their basic needs. They still need you to be that ATM machine for as long as possible. In my case my lawyer got my alimony capped at 6 years!

You need to be prepared for all of this just in case it goes down in exactly the manner in which I described. For me it did exactly that, and just like when we were married, they are thankless in the fact that I am still providing for most of basics which they require to maintain a lifestyle of their choosing.

No one knows to what degree your life will be impacted. There is always a chance that it could even be worse than I described. Do not be surprised if your spouse turns mid-evil on you, wishing you would suffer a long and painful existence. They may want to try and saddle you with all the debts that currently exist in the marriage. Debt that could take years to completely pay off. They may try to convince your children that you did things which they have no proof of. Many would like nothing more than to punish you by whatever means, as I can attest to.

Is it Already Too Late

Based on the severity of neglect that one spouse has for the other can determine if the relationship has reached the point of no return. Don't be afraid to admit the presence of any emotional vulnerability. This is the time where you need to be open with your feelings. Suppressing your feelings can only create anxiety, even hatred that you might be feeling for your spouse.

When you open emotionally you start to reconnect with your spouse at a deeper connection and understanding. When you embrace each other's vulnerabilities, you begin to transform back to the couple you once were. Over time, addressing the vulnerabilities fosters empathy and builds emotional intimacy. The emotional component is only half of the equation. Then there is the physical component of the relationship.

No one can deny that physical contact can help ignite emotional intimacy, as we have already proven. Those simple acts that you saw in other couples holding hands is that catalyst for turning around your whole self-worth and feelings you have for your partner. Frequent hugging or cuddling up to watch a romantic movie generates feelings of closeness and safety.

Your relationship may have gotten to the point where each party is casting blame on the other. This is the first sign that the relationship maybe too damaged to be repaired, that one or both of you have given up on even attempting to repair the relationship. Unless both of you want to reconcile your differences, then it makes little sense to try and save your marriage because each one of you are already admitting you are heading in opposite directions. However, if there is still a little fight in both of you, enough to want to rekindle that spark you once had for each other then you must learn to compromise. Rebuilding the intimacy in your relationship takes time, it takes patient, but most importantly, it takes both of you. If you both don't want to work towards rebuilding your relationship, then there is no real relationship left to rebuild. Don't try to hold onto what has already long been gone.

Lack of Physical Intimacy

Most experts will agree that one of the top reason for divorce is the lack of intimacy in the marriage. Others include too much conflict and arguing, and lack of commitment. It does not take a brain surgeon, or multiple studies to tell me that not having these things in your relationship is never a good thing, and prolonged exposure causes irreputable damage to the relationship. One may choose to ignore it, but deep down we know what is going on, or shall I say what is not going on is not healthy for either of you. [3-1]

Throughout our lives, we have all experienced in one form or another, a relationship where there is a lot of intimacy: emotional as well as the physical, and those have probably been successful and satisfying relationships. I am also sure that most of us have experienced the other side where there is a lack of emotional and physical intimacy. Over time there is a void which is created by this lack of intimacy and it continues to expand over time. This leaves individuals feeling disconnected and unfulfilled in the relationship.

When looking at successful relationships you will surely find a strong rich sensitivity between the couple. They care for each other; they look out for their partners mental health and physical well-being.

When you or your spouse comes home from a rough day on the job, does the other try and relieve the frustration or stress from the day by offering a simple gesture? Like "do you want to talk about it," maybe offer a neck message, or share a glass of wine together. These gestures are a clear sign that the person cares about the other and is bothered that their spouse has had a difficult day. They want to do what they can to make the end of the night something good to remember. They are saddened by their spouse being upset.

Holding hands, hugging, cuddling, and those deep gazes into each other's eyes, are obvious signs of the emotional closeness that two people have for each other. These small gestures are clearly not sexual in nature, but they can warm the heart just the same. These everyday gestures are the foundation of the relationship. Add in a physical closeness in sharing one's love for each other, and you have the makings of a deep lasting relationship.

We see examples of this on an everyday basis. You can be walking in the park or along the shoreline on a beautiful sunshining day and see two complete strangers walking towards you. As they get closer you tell the couple are involved and have a close intimacy about them. The couple are holding hands, being very engaging in eye contact, smiling, even laughing. All the signs of a healthy physical relationship. Couples which are walking side-by-side, but lack the physical contact or verbal conversation, are more likely to have a lessor physical relationship, and hence a degree of concern or stress added into their relationship. I'm not saying they are less in love with each other but the chemistry of these two relationships is different.

Relationships are in a constant state of evolution. You may start to notice small subtle changes that are affecting the relationship. This could be caused by the rigors of life in general, however, you should always be concerned. If your spouse is dealing with a demanding situation, then they could use some comforting. If they seem to be taking a negative tone with you, then you may want to pay closer attention. You will need to determine if these are becoming more frequent in nature, as these could be a sign that there is tension festering between the two of you.

Be advised, you do not want to let these things go unnoticed or ignore them completely. If you push them aside for too long, you may wake up one day and that person you call your spouse may not be the same person you thought you married. When you start to lose the emotional & physical bonds which you once enjoyed, your relationship will suffer. Studies have shown that when intimacy is taken out of a relationship it leads to emotional detachment and negative feelings. This breakdown in the relationship affects both the mental as well as physical well-being. If the actions continue in this negative direction, you will surely get to the point where the relationship runs the risk of breaking down completely.

The lack of physical intimacy in a relationship can led to a breakdown in communication and create an emotional distancing between you and your spouse. Over time, this void becomes increasingly difficult to bridge, leaving individuals feeling disconnected and unfulfilled in the relationship.

Furthermore, the absence of physical intimacy can create low self-esteem and a lack of self-worth. Science has proven that the human touch releases oxytocin, often called the "love hormone," crucial in fostering feelings of bonding and security. Without regular doses of this "physically intimate" hormone, individuals may experience a decline in their overall wellness, leading to increased stress, anxiety, and even depression.

Moreover, the lack of physical intimacy can also manifest in other areas of the relationship. It can give rise to resentment, frustration, and a sense of unmet needs. In some cases, individuals may seek fulfillment outside the relationship, leading to infidelity or a breakdown in trust. Thus, the repercussions of neglecting physical intimacy in a relationship can extend far beyond the bedroom and permeating into all aspects of a couple's life.

Studies have proven that the lack of emotional connection can profoundly impact sexual intimacy within a marriage. Emotional connection serves as the foundation for a healthy and satisfying sexual relationship, as it fosters trust, vulnerability, and open communication between partners.

- *When couples struggle to establish or maintain this emotional bond, it becomes increasingly challenging to bridge the gap in their sexual connection.*

- *Without deeply understanding each other's desires, needs, and emotional state, partners may struggle to express their true selves and experience genuine intimacy.*

- *The absence of emotional connection can lead to feelings of detachment, dissatisfaction, and a lack of fulfillment in the bedroom, causing strain and frustration within the marriage.*

Addressing and nurturing the emotional connection between partners is crucial for fostering a fulfilling sexual relationship that thrives on trust, understanding, affection, and mutual satisfaction. [3-2]

Uncontrolled Spending

As if the lack of physical attention towards me was not enough for any spouse to handle, there was the constant outflow of cash; and the mountain of credit card debt that never seemed to stop. Being the sole supporter of the family, I was left alone, having to fight this losing battle of holding my family above water and managing all the finances. As the debt rose, so did my level of stress and anxiety. Most of the time there was no relief in sight. The sad part about this was that no one in the family cared about the effect of all that stress and anxiety was having on my physical and mental health.

I continued to provide for the family while they kept spending. At the rate we were spending it was clear that one solution which could at least eliminate the negative cash flow each month was my spouse going back into to work. We must have had that conversation at least a dozen times and it always ended abruptly with her not even entertaining the idea of working again. It did not matter to her that her husband was virtually begging her for help, some kind of lifeline, so we could turn this around. It did not matter that I reconciled every credit card and bank statement spending activity to show her exactly how much was being spent; and she simply ignored them.

She had a good thing going, a nice comfortable life, and she did not want anything to change that, especially having to get a job. I also had no say in my kids' lives; not when they were under the age of eighteen, and when they all were still living in our house, well into their twenties.

It's your job as a parent to prepare your children for what they will face when they must go out into the world and have to face these challenges head on. All my attempts to prepare our children for that day, met with heavy resistance from their mother. My ex was right behind me contradicting everything I said. I tried to have them take on paying for some of their own expenses as they moved into their twenties, but my wife would have nothing of the sort by telling them they did not have to pay for a thing. I was just a paycheck, a person that provided them the means to have a lifestyle that my salary and debt load could not afford. In their fantasy world, I had an endless supply of riches buried somewhere in the backyard or was it in the walls of our house somewhere, as my spouse accused me of once doing. She even convinced the kids that it was true.

As the years passed nothing changed, in fact it got worse each year. Our credit card debt skyrocketed to almost six figures. The interest alone was a small mortgage payment for most people. This was not the first time that our debt rose out of control. A few years prior, we were facing similar debts. I was able to dig my way out of the debt completely in only a few years. At that time, having a successful business afford me a bonus every so often. They were never intended to be used to catch-up on our debts. They should have been used to build a college fund for the kids and save some for my eventual retirement.

The sad part was that no one in the family seemed to care one way or the other. They did not care about the escalating stress & anxiety that was strangling me. As far as they were concerned these were all my problem to solve. I was having chest pains, just thinking of how I was going to pay for all. By taking advantage of some money management strategies, I was able to barely keep pace with making the minimum payments and interest on the credit cards. I leveraged some good ole credit card swaps, transferring high interest debt to no interest credit cards, while trying cutting costs everything that I could.

When I was finally able to pull us out from under all that debt, the levels of stress and anxiety that I was feeling was greatly reduced. What I did not count on was that while I was looking to save and stretch every dollar, my spouse never altered her spending habits. The expenditures continued to exceed my monthly income. This started the debt and interest to start to climb again. In less than twelve months our debt was approaching the mid five figure range, yet again. I felt that I had barely blinked, and we were heading right back to where we were such a short time ago. Once again, no one really cared, it was as always, back on my shoulders to worry about. It was at this point that I had to be brutally honest with myself.

I was 59 years old, married thirty-one years and finally woke up. I realized that things would never change, and it scared me in a huge way. Scared that I would wake up one day with a mountain of debt and being too old to be able to support myself or my family. I would have a limited retirement saved, and unable to even think about retiring. As people around me started to talk about retirement and how they were going to spend it, I was living in fear of what that future would look like for me. I had an incredibly good career run for over thirty-eight years, yet little to show for it when it came to my retirement fund. This had a paralyzing effect on me.

I had an insanely high monthly mortgage and due to a refinance, this mortgage wouldn't be paid off for another eighteen years; putting me at almost eighty years of age. I realized that the only way that I would be able to pay off the mortgage is if my death benefits kicked in. Even with that, my family might not be debt free. I just could not live the remainder of my life this way. It was too depressing to think about. Talk about a life sentence with no hopes of parole; this was my life. I could not continue down this road any longer. In February 2022, both parties signed the divorce papers.

I am hoping that I have opened your eyes a bit and shown you things that might not have been so obvious. Things that if you are not aware of them could create problems for you during this journey. As my dad always said, prepare for the worst and hope for the best. Take nothing for granted, assume nothing and you will be better off.

Accusations

Remember this is a divorce, and in most of the cases, a full-blown trial is not in your future, more on your options later. If you are unable to afford the five figure costs of going to trial, only the judge or mediator will hear what you have to say. You might also be limited in the amount of time in which to defend your case, while disputing your spouse's claims. If you are ever

If you are the husband, you are starting with two strikes against you. Hey, that is just the way the court system is wired in today's world. Divorce courts tend to side with the wife, especially if there are children involved. Her lawyers will take whatever pieces of facts they can find and create a story around them which is just plausible enough to be believed, regardless of if it's true or not. I can guarantee you that this will not be a picture that paints you in a favorable light.

They don't even need the proof to back up these false claims and accusations. That is just how the system works. It's equivalent to what you hear on TV programs. We have heard it a dozens of times. Where the lawyer says some outrageous statement, the other side objects, and the judge asks the jury to disregard the entire statement. As normal human beings how can we "unhear" something. When you think about it, it's pretty ridiculous.

In my case it was alluded to that all the hours of overtime, and late nights at my clients' offices; weeks in a hotel room stuck in places like, Wichita, Kansas, was in fact not spent working, but was spent fooling around with my co-workers, clients, and complete strangers. All without having any proof of such actions. Not one witness to collaborate their story. The only true part of this tail was that I did have to spend many a night in hotel rooms, actually over one thousand nights spent in hotel rooms, over a twenty-five year career.

My ex got the mediating judge to buy into this ridiculous nonsense. When it came to my time to dispute all the details of the stories, he was in the mindset to hear none of my rebuttal to these false accusations. From that point forward, they spent the next five hours carving me up like a Thanksgiving turkey. Taking everything they could away from me!

Her lawyers supported her lies and accusations, their angle the entire time was that if it seemed plausible to the average person then it must be true. She got them all, including my own children to believe that I had all these affairs over the last ten years of our marriage, and that I was not in fact working all those hours. If I wasn't working all those hours, how was I able to provide them with the lifestyle that they all enjoyed. How would it be that my daughter got to attend one of the best Universities in the country when it came to their theatre and art program. I'm surprised they didn't make up some story of me robbing banks in my spare time, maybe I simply printed the extra money on my LaserJet printer, or maybe I sold my baseball cards for millions of dollars.

If you're thinking that his is not going to happen to you, wouldn't you rather be prepared for the unthinkable, just in case it does? I really hope that our relationship with your ex results in an uneventful series of events that leads to a quick and amicable divorce settlement. I know sure wasn't the situation that I had to deal with for some eighteen months.

My ex could have been a magician. She conducted a masterful performance, intent on crushing me into the ground, despite the lack of having the facts to back up her accusations. She got all of her family, friends & our children to believe all of it. In the process she also wanted to receive a settlement where she would still be living her life at my expense, having received enough alimony so that she wouldn't have to go back to work. I know that she sure got a big enough monthly check for the average person to not have to work.

Her performances were masterful, she had so many fooled into believing her false tails. I wish it were all a dream, instead I was living through my worst nightmare. Her whole pitch was that since I had the opportunity and the means to cheat, meant that I did cheat. She never substantiated any of her claims. She never provided any shred of evidence proving her allegations. In the process her implications damaged my reputation in the business world as those accusations were told to two people, who told it to two more people, and on and on. It is pathetic, probably more sickening that she sold these lies and exaggerations to our own children. Driving a wedge between myself and our children.

During my lifetime I have always tried to be nice to people where others might simply look the other way. I try to help others when I was fortunate enough to be able to afford to be thankful and pay it forward to others who may be struggling. During my divorce I was found guilty of caring for people, wanting to help people in need, people suffering through tough times, people that just needed a little glimmer of hope that their lives could turn around.

Yes, I gave money to a family in need. In this particular case I thought that if I could do good for someone else, changing their life for the better while my life was falling apart, that in some way it would make me feel better. Knowing that the money went to turning around an entire extended family, meant so much more than some needless "stuff" that was bought instead. All too often, all too much of my paycheck was used for the extra things in life that were not really necessary. Was it necessary to spend well over $750,000 dollars on a house on the side of a ski mountain in Vermont? No it wasn't, and I made it possible, I let it happen.

I never thought my ex was that greedy, that selfish, and would be that enraged with jealousy around the entire thing. When I married her, she was far from being the one not to care about others, nor was she self-centered in any way. But as the years went by she changed. hanged her. I could not provide her the fairy tale life that she dreamt up in her mind, she got nastier to other people who she felt threatened by. During the marriage, I did not realize the transformation that she was undergoing, the more success I was having, the more greedy, selfish, and spiteful she became. She wanted to live a fantasy life of the rich and famous. No matter how much money I would have been able to earn it would not have been enough for her.

She took any means necessary to spin anything she could in a negative light, trying to lay the blame for everything bad that happened to our family and our marriage squarely on my shoulders. She played the martyr role very well during all of this. She could not get past the fact that there were no extra marital affairs, there was no house or apartments that I owned, and there was no secret second family living in Romania. But that did not stop her from making up stories saying that these ridiculous things actually took place. It was an opportunity she saw to better her financial situation, while punishing me in the process. I made one family's lives better, giving them hope, and maybe a foundation to build upon into the future. Nothing different than I had done for dozens of people before them. I even gave my ex's best friends husband a chance at building a new career with my company when it looked like he was lined up for a round of downsizing at his former company. I guess giving him a compensation package of three times what I gave that family was OK, since it was her best friend's family that I was taking care of. By the way he worked for me for over five years, totaled well over ten times that of anything I did for almost any of my other employees. I wonder why my ex didn't complain about any of this.

My wife stopped loving me long before we started divorce proceedings, more than a decade to be precise. Do not do what I did, do not let ten years pass you by when you could have gotten on with your life well before that. Do not ignore what is happening around you. Do not try to hold onto what is already gone!

I waited way to long and what was my reward? My wife told our children lies and fairy tales of a mysterious life that I was living since 2009. She told these stories over years and years, taking every opportunity to undermine me in any way that she could. She took conversations off my phone and laptop in the middle of the night while I was asleep; a lot of meaningless banter that and taken completely out of context and used to try and support her false stories. Greed and vengeance drove her quest to destroy me.

I was even accused of a sexual affair at a local municipal airport, on Christmas Eve; REALLY? Then she made up the story of me having a house and a second family outside of the U.S. Not sure when I had the time for all that nonsense, having worked upward of three thousand hours in that year. She did all of this without having to produce even one shred of evidence which would corroborate her stories. You wonder why? Because she made them all up, they never actually happened. If she had any evidence, she would have gladly volunteered it to her lawyers.

In the end she got virtually all our assets and while I got almost all of our debts. She lied for financial gain. For eighteen months she spun her web of lies and deceit, she fooled her lawyers, and she fooled the courts mediator assigned to our case. Oh, and in the process, she scarred our children in the process.

Lack of Support

Not only did we not have any physical contact during the last decade of our marriage, but she also made sure that whenever I tried to have conversations with her or anyone else. She would go out of her way to correct me, call me a liar, accuse me of never being able to remember the facts, or straight out contradict me. She did this regardless of the company that was in the room at the time. [3-3]

Our children got to see, firsthand, the total disregard she had in respecting anything I said or did during those last ten years. This abuse and head games went on, non-stop. It was abundantly clear that she wanted nothing to do with me. At every turn, when alone with me, with the kids present, or even friends and family around, she made sure to continue the verbally assaulting, condescending, and contradictory attitude toward me. It didn't matter how disrespectful it was or how seemingly pathetic it made me look, the badgering continued with reckless abandon.

My spouse treated me as if I was somehow not capable of having a normal relationship, that I somehow had the early stages of dementia, or something. She laid the foundation for my children that included little to no respect for me. They only did what their mother told them. When I asked them to do something, it was greeted with resentment and disregard. They often ignored my requests or went to their mother for validation.

This is not how a marriage should work; this is not how parenting should work and this is certainly not how children should communicate with their father. There should not be a "he said/she said" battle every time disagreements occur. Parents should have a united front when it comes to how their children are raised. This was hard for me to manage, it seemed that with each passing day my input as a parent was more and more ignored. From the time our first son was born, I have dedicated myself to taking care of my children, keeping my children safe, and improving their lives. I tried to make sure that they had opportunities that others might not have. Opportunities which I never had. I made sacrifices for them without hesitation, without remorse. To me, this is part of the responsibilities of being a parent.

It was impossible to imagine, I would wake up to realize that my spouse had been executing her on own agenda, with little regard for anyone else. The worst part of this was to realize how deep the brainwashing had gone. Even though I tried my hardest to improve my standing with my kids, the damage was already done. All of my ex's tirades, accusations, and lies framed me as a monster in my children's eyes. The worst feeling, I have ever had or will ever have in my lifetime.

To be treated like this day in and day out, was much worse than any prison could dish out. Not that I know first-hand, but in prison you do have all sorts of people trying to break you down. However, the one thing that inmates have in their favor, is usually the support of their families, friends and loved ones. People need hope in desperate times. When there is no hope, then what is there left to look forward to? What is there to live for? Ya, most people saw me living in a big house with a nice lawn and beautiful swimming pool, but what they didn't see, was that I was trapped inside, prisoner, with little hope for parole, and no family to support me.

Conclusion / Lessons Learned

I understand if there are some of you who are thinking that all these things could not happen to just one person, but it's all true. It's only some of the torment that fathers must endure because of society putting much of the responsibility in supporting and keeping safe, their family. Remember:

- Money isn't everything. Money is not the end goal. Money can't buy happiness and most of all, if you are going to "go for it", remember at what price you may have to pay. Losing out on a lot of family's memories, and the events that are important to your children. I learned this lesson the hard way. I just wish I could turn back time.

- Don't regret following your heart. If you want to help others because you feel it is the right thing to do, then make it happen. Being able to change someone's life is an incredible feeling.

- You and your spouse must be on the same page concerning your financial goals. Both spouses must sit down together, make a budget, and stick to it. You cannot be going in opposite directions. If you do, then your relationship is doomed to failure.

- During your marriage outside focuses can derail your relationship. Address these as they happen. Do not ignore them, do not dismiss them. These things have a habit of escalating.

- If you are sitting on the fence about, should you or should you not be getting a divorce, then you probably have already made that decision. Be fair to yourself when taking stock of the current state of your marriage. Can you continue to live your life in this manner, while feeling good about ourselves? If you are having serious doubts, don't dismiss them, address them, or prepare yourself to deal with them with lawyers.

Chapter-III: Believing in Yourself

I always knew that I was a little different from the other kids in the neighborhood. My mind was always racing, looking around the corner to see what could be coming next. I was a typical dreamer. Little did I know was that being ADHD didn't allow my mind to slow down and process things in a serial manner. It was natural for me to be thinking about a half-dozen things at one time, instead of just one or two.

When I was only twelve I got five dollar weekly allowance. In 1974 five dollar went a lot farther than it does today! However, it still was only five dollars, and I knew having more money equaled freedom & flexibility, and definitely more pizza. You see back in the 70's Long Island, New York was not as developed as it is today. The "gang" would ride our bikes through the woods, a little over a mile, and we would come out behind the local pizzeria/deli. It was the only one around. In our eyes it carried everything anyone could ask for. It was awesome.

I knew that I could have so much more fun with twenty dollars than with only five dollars. I was confident that this goal was achievable, but of course I had no idea how to go about it. I did not get ten feet into my driveway when I heard my dad yell out, "before you think about going anywhere else you better get that grass cut." I thought to myself, why not do for others what I did around my house and get paid for it. As I got to the shed to get the lawn mower it hit me. I could start cutting the neighbors lawns, charging five dollars per lawn. Since I did not have a driver's license, I was only able to do the houses in my neighborhood. My route grew quickly, requiring me to enlisting the driving services of my mom and our Vista Cruiser station wagon. My landscaping business afforded me a job where the pay was better than working for someone else and allotted me freedom to make my own hours.

I have always loved creating something from scratch, working hard to deliver high valued, customer service, then expanded the business organically. I also loved the idea that I was working the same hours as my friends but was taking home three times the money. It was also an all-cash business, which made a difference as I got much older and the business started to grow.

Being a young entrepreneur, I could say that most of the people I knew, which included friends and family did not believe that my businesses would survive. They even mocked me. This gave more motivation to prove them wrong, which in most cases I did. I also hired a few of my friends, and at that point they were no longer laughing.

Even after I graduated college and started my career with computers, I could not shake being in business for myself. I finally handed over all my landscaping accounts to two of my friends. I knew it was about time to put all my focus on my computer career. I will say, once an entrepreneur always an entrepreneur. It's in your blood. It's exciting and filled with unknow adventure.

During the tenure at my second computer job, I got that urge again to start up a venture with a friend of mine. This time it was a bar. What set of twenty-four year olds do you know that go out on their own and by a bar. It was crazy, but I will admit it was pretty cool at that. The place was located in Levittown, Long Island, New York. It featured live music on the weekends. Unlike my landscaping business this business came with a lot of overhead. I had to worry about getting a liquor license, paying rent, managing the employees, and watching the cash. I remember being only twenty-four and having all this responsibility and all these obligations. Even though I lasted only one year, before selling, it felt like five. I ended up breaking about even. I was able to payback all the seed money that I borrowed from my dad. I also walked away learning so much about how to run a real business, and maybe more importantly, how not to run a business. Believe me there is a lot to be learned from failing. As long as you recognize it quickly and create a plan to turn the ship and head into calmer sees, you will be successful. A lesson that was later reinforced at the General Electric company. The company that I'm still employed as of today.

Go with What Works

Once I had three to four years of experience in the financial software technology arena, I branched out on my own. Yep, I started yet again, another company. This time there was serious money to be made. At first, I was an independent consultant, working long hours, bringing in a lot more as a consultant then I did when I was as an employee of the bank. I had this knack for fixing customers problems where many other consultants had failed. On my first project as my own company, a company of one, I was added to a projects with other software developers for a Fortune-25 company. It didn't take long before the client recognized my contributions. I believe in rather than charging a high hourly rate, I would rather deliver high value at a discounted rate. This way they would keep me on the project longer. In this case my cost to the client was almost half the hourly rate of the other consulting firms, and I delivery almost twice the output of work.

A few months passed when they approached me asking me if I had any other employees that I could bring onto the project? I just smiled and replied, "of course I do". Unofficially, at that exact moment I did not have any official employees, but I had floated the idea past a few friends and people I had worked with before.

This was the catalyst I needed to take the business from a single employee consulting programming service to a full-fledged company. I went to a coworker from the prior company that I worked for and asked him if he wanted to take a chance and come work for me. He was impressed that I landed such a large client.

P a g e | 50

Having that one client allowed me to bring on three more employees.

To ensure my new employees were happy with their new jobs, I made sure that everyone was making well over what their previous corporate jobs were paying them. This allowed me the peace of mind that none of them would leave to springboard over to another company. Everyone was getting a sizable quarterly bonus, determined by the number of hours they were generating revenue. We were having a great time. I was proud of my accomplishments and the good I was doing for my friends.

My approach to setting our hourly rates for our employees was paying off. I believed that delivering high valued work at a fair price and forego profits would result in a deeper relationship of trust with our clients. This also resulting in longer engagements for our employees. None of our employees were ever on the bench. This allowed us to add two more employees during the first two years. I have to say it felt great leading a growing company and it felt even better being able to improve the lives of our employees.

All along my spouse was reaping the rewards from each of my bonuses. We were able to move out of our first starter house on Long Island, New York, into a much larger, roomier house with a lot more land in Sandy Hook, Connecticut.

With the company running at over one hundred percent capacity with seven employees it was getting hard to keep up with client demands for our services and the operations of the company. My spouse at that time, was running the back office, for which I was paying her a salary, but the amount of client tracking, invoicing, employee payroll, health insurance and other back office operations, was getting too much for one person to handle. It was time to bring on a second person. This allowed for the back office to once again run smoothly. I was able to focus more on revenue generating and client relations activities, while continue to bill myself out. Two activities that were my specialty.

I knew I wanted to grow the company, but I also knew I was working at over one hundred percent of the normal amount of a fulltime consultant. Maybe it was my ambition to succeed and grow the business, and maybe part of me was chasing a larger paycheck so I could provide better for my family. Nonetheless, I couldn't keep up this pace.

It was time to take on a partner, but I needed the right person that would mix well with my challenges that having ADHD generated. When I was consulting for the vendor of the software, I met Andy, a down to earth guy, who also had a similar intense drive to succeed, as I did. During our tenure at the software company Andy and I generated the most revenue and racked up the most billable hours of any consultants in the New York Metro area of anyone in the company at the time. We were Top-10 across all of the consultants in the company.

It just so happens that Andy formed his own consulting company during the same year as I started mine. We both were struggling with keeping up with the growth of building a successful company. At that point, it made sense to merge the two companies. We created Pinnacle. Andy was a fantastic business partner and good friend. We had each other's backs, we knew each other's strengths and weaknesses, our likes, and dislikes. We were able to manage conflict in a swift amicable way. The new joint company delivered all that we hoped it would.

My wife on the other hand, hated the idea of merging the two companies. She hated the idea of Andy and I splitting ownership of the company fifty-fifty. This did not sit well with her as she was feeling the sense of losing control. Control that was only in her imagination because she did not have any official decision-making authority as she owned no shares in the company. Merging would in affect eliminate her influence on the business, as she would no longer be responsible for the back office operations. Andy made clear that it was unfair that we have joint ownership and then to pay my spouse additional compensation on top of my own. I couldn't really disagree with his argument. It was also a way for him to eliminate her from the equation and not have to deal with a situation where multiple people would be ganging up against him. Making those concessions was necessary to make the merger happen. It solved several challenges that we were struggling with as separate companies.

Our validation came almost immediately. With Andy driving client relationships and new business, while I managed employees, company operations and project ad-on work. We were like two large overlapping circles that barely crossed. This afforded us the maximum coverage across all the areas of our business. In 2006 we landed Pinnacle as #157 of 500 on Inc Magazines America's Fast Growing Companies list. That was my second time that I landed a company on the list. The first time was with my pre-merger company Lindin Consulting. It was great to get recognized for all our hard work by a reputable publication like Inc Magazine.

However, I could see the festering resentment that was building inside my spouse. She was resenting the success, even though she was indirectly benefitting from it all. This further put stress on our already struggling marriage.

Sharing the Wealth

I think most of us have heard the term, "paying it forward"! To me that's having the means and/or ability to help others less fortunate than ourselves when we have good fortunate shine our way. It really has nothing to do with if you are rich or not. What kind of house you live or what kind of car you drive. It's about realizing when good fortunes shine on us it's not by chance. You need to recognize this; you need to do the right thing by others.

For as long as I can remember I realized I like to leave things better off than when I found them. I liked helping people, it makes me feel really good seeing how I was able to make a difference in people's lives. I enjoy seeing people smile after they have been through tough times, or maybe just a tough day.

Even though I may be facing challenges of my own, I try and give back a minimum of a small piece of my time to others. After I graduated from college, finding a job was not easy. I could not find the right fit. I was unable to make that connection with my future employer. Then one interview it was going better than the others when my prospective boss, blurted out, "I know your father, he really knows his computers!" referencing the computer books my dad had authored. He then asked me why I wanted this job? I replied that I loved working with computers and felt I had a lot to offer, if I was only given the chance. He had his reasons and hired me when all others would not. I will not ever forget what this man did for me. He paid it forward to me, and I knew that I would do the same one day.

After only six months of starting this job, they announced that they sold the company and were moving to New Jersey. I was cool with having to move to New Jersey and was excited about the opportunity. Right up to the time that I realized that this opportunity did not include myself, as I was too junior in the role I had. I was a bit depressed about the fact that I would be unemployed in the coming months. It took a while before I landed a position at one of the top banks in the country, Chase Manhattan Bank. This job and the next three jobs, all seemed to stall after about eighteen months. I realize that my ADHD was a driving force that gave me a challenge in moving forward in the job.

However, I did gain valuable experience from these opportunities. Enough to start my own company LINDIN consulting, a technology consulting firm. Through some friends and work connections I was able to land one of the largest telecommunication companies in the country as my first client. This funded the business growth for the next few years. It also required me to hire my first few employees. LINDIN later merged to form Pinnacle.

I'm a firm believer in loyalty, and my first three hires were people I worked with at my prior jobs. The fourth, being my ex's lifelong best friend's husband. He was in fear of being downsized from one of the largest reinsurance firms in the United States. He was an accountant but knew nothing about the software for which I provided services. I told him if he could commit the time, I could train him on the software. He agreed. I knew he was a bright guy, and particularly good with people, so I made the investment in hiring him. To ensure that he would be comfortable with the opportunity, I gave him quite a large raise over what his former employer was paying him. Even though it would cost me over two hundred thousand dollars per year, I felt I should take my good fortune and share the wealth. He stayed with the company until it was sold, then he went to work fulltime for one of my clients.

Things were all working according to plan and the business was growing. I felt very thankful for my success. Being able to help others is something I'm still very proud of. In the beginning my ex was all in agreement that we should share our good fortune, at least in the beginning.

At that time, we participated in the Letters-to-Santa, "Operation Santa" program which the United States Post Office initiated in 1912. The first Santa's mailroom was created by the Postmaster General. He authorized local postmaster to open these letters for employees to read and respond to them. Well, that tradition exploded and continues today. Last year alone, an estimated twenty million letters were received at the main USPS location. Ordinary folks, like you and me, can go down to your local post office and ask to see these letters. You are allowed to take them home and reply to them in the way was you see fit. As long it was within the Letters-To-Santa postal guidelines. Approximately one hundred thousand letters are responded to by ordinary citizens, from the Manhattan Post office alone.

There were some letters which were requests from children for elaborate gifts like a sports car, or a wish for money. These letters were returned to the Post Office. The remaining letters were ones of desperation. Stories of hardships which most of us have never had to live through. My ex and I used to go into New York City a week or two before Christmas to sift through the tens of thousands of letters. The first year we did this we pulled out five or six letters, then with each passing year we would pull increasingly more letters to reply to.

These letters just broke my heart, it was very emotional to read them as I could feel their pain through their words. One was from the oldest child of four, two brothers and a sister. All he asked for were socks for his brothers and sister, as it got cold in their apartment that had little heat in the winter months. I remember shopping for members of my own family and all I could think of was this boy and his only wish for Christmas was to keep his siblings warm for the winter. Fortunately, he left an address, so we were able to send him enough socks for all of his family.

Another letter was a little girl asking for a small stuffed animal to replace the one her baby sister had lost, as she had trouble going to sleep without it. The thing about young children is they are straight forward and forth coming with their assessment of things, as they understand them. They tell it like it is. Reading these letters, you knew they were not scams, they were not greedy people trying to take advantage of others kindness. They were ordinary people, innocent children thrown into adult situations, which they should have never had to deal with in the first place. In despair they reached out for help to the one man that never let them down, Santa.

I would be surprised if most of the post offices around the country do not have programs like this one by now. I highly recommend you take time out of your schedule and get involved. It was a humbling experience, but also an experience to be proud of. Answer just one letter and it will change you forever.

We continued this tradition for many years, it was part of our holiday season. At one point we brought back five letters for each of our employees so that they could live the experience firsthand. We gave each of them five hundred dollars to spend on playing Santa for a day. A few of the employees came back to us and told us the stories of people that they had helped, while others kept it private. I was proud to have set up and supported a program like that in my own company. I think all too often many of us go through life and don't realize how fortunate we are. We sometimes forget how hard it can get, and what if we never got that helping hand when we needed it most. Think of all the times that you must be thankful to someone else, especially if it was a stranger. Remember no matter how hard of a year you have had, there are hundreds of people in your community which have had similar or worse experiences.

Doing the Right Thing

Over the course of my career, I have always thrown myself into my work. I also try and get the people I work with to be engaged and interested in the projects and jobs that we do. It makes it for a more effective and rewarding experience all around. It's also about treating people with respect, treating people like they are family (in a good way).

Our business relied on having and keeping top consulting talent. The competition for resources was viscous. Companies were throwing around money left and right to virtually any resource that had five years of practical experience. We knew we had to give our employees an incentive to stay with us.

We valued the people who worked for us. We were mostly a service provider where hours worked at the customer was our revenue stream. In other words, our employees that were out in the field were vital to the success and growth of our company. Andy and I had a closer relationship to our team then most companies would typically have with their employees. We wanted to reward them for their past loyalty while giving them the incentive to stick with us moving into the future. Andy and I decided to give back to the employees, fifteen percent of the net proceeds of the company to all of the employees, if we were to ever sell the company. To Andy and I this made perfect sense, but so many other people thought we were crazy to give all that money away. To me and Andy it was more like sharing our good fortune with our work family.

As part of everyone's employment agreement was a generous one-time bonus if we would ever sell our company. The only requirement was that you had to be employed as of the date of closing of the sale. Well, in 2008, the day came where we did in fact sell the company. Looking back, it was not the greatest of deals, as they say, hindsight is 20/20. On the day of closing the employees which stuck with us, all received their share from the proceeds of the sale of the company, totaling close to $850,000.

To this day when I hook up with some of our former employees, they mention the fact that they still cannot believe we did not try to get out of our agreement. Many told us how the unexpected bonus allowed for them to do things they always wanted to do with their lives. Take that dream vacation they had been trying to save for or eliminating the debt they had been carrying for years or putting away for their kids' education. I think I can speak for my partner when I say we were extremely proud of our work family and excited that we could share our good fortune with them.

One day I received some very disturbing news. One of our coworkers, a member of the Lindin and Pinnacle family, and close personal friend, had suddenly passed away. While attending his wake, his mother came up to me and introduced herself. She thanked me for giving her son an opportunity. One that changed his direction and path in life. Dejean was a good man, a man I considered my friend, may he rest in eternal peace.

That same day, another employee sat down next to me and we started talking about old times. He recalled the first client that I assigned him. He recalls going in knowing little about our technology, and remembers that I had complete, unwavering confidence in him that he would be successful. We both laughed at the antics which took place on that project. It was crazy but rewarding in so many ways. I then asked him for a small favor and his reply left me in silence.

He replied, "Mike, you just name it, you gave me the opportunity that others wouldn't, you changed my life forever!" I was touched by his kind words. A memory that will stay with me for the rest of my life. He made me realize how much good I had done for so many. Many of them whom I barely knew at the time.

Bottom line: I was raised with the belief that I could make a positive difference in other people's lives if given the chance. Having my own company afforded me the means to help others. I worked side-by-side with many of my employees. Many days we worked well into the night and on occasion we worked through the night and into the next day. Even though these people were all my employees, I considered them my friends and part of my family.

Conclusion / Lessons Learned

- Know your strengths. This includes knowing the conditions which you perform best under. If you want to succeed you have to position yourself in a setting that will help you achieve your goals. Then you have to believe in yourself that you can handle the challenges that loom ahead.

- Follow your intuition. Know that you can handle this regardless of what others may think or say to you.

- Most people have heard the term "what goes around comes around." Keep this in the back of your mind when you are working with other people. Treat people with respect and they will most likely treat you with respect back. In general be kind to people. If you're having a bad day, don't take it out on others who had nothing to do with you having a bad day. Instead do something nice for others could actually turn your bad day around.

- Many of us have had the light of good fortune shine on us. Remember that things happen for a reason and that we all need to do our part in sharing our good fortune with others. It can be something small, do good deeds by others, it will come back to you multi-fold.

- Do right by what you feel in your heart. It might not be the most popular thing, or the most obvious thing, but if you feel that it is the right thing to do, then just do it! If you follow your heart you can never go wrong.

Chapter-IV: The Tipping Point

The Tipping Point is used to describe the point in time, and / or the event that catapulted your life, relationship or business exponentially in one direction or the other. For me, in my life, the tipping point, was when I realized my life, my company, and my marriage was drastically changing.

In the latter part of 2007 and into 2008 the United States suffered through a financial crisis which impacted almost every large organization. In a relatively short period of time the panic spread across every industry. Resulting in a hoarding frenzy for cash. Companies were putting projects on hold or cancelling them altogether. As we were a service company and our customers were all from the finance departments of these large organizations which were hit the hardest, our revenue stream was immediately impacted. Our pipeline, identifying new project all but dried up overnight. We did not have much time to react. To the point that for the first time in almost ten years we were in jeopardy of not being able to make our payroll commitment. Now a 50-person company, the banks were not looking at us as a good candidate for a bridge loan, which would have held us over until the crisis subsided.

For Andy and I this was the tipping point that went in the negative direction. However, we tried to look at this as an opportunity. Just prior to the full-blown impact across all of the major industries was an event which provided us a possible way to sell our company to a suitor that would allow us to growth the company further. The software company that owned the products which our company provided services for, was being bought out my an even larger software firm. This meant that companies specializing in the larger companies' software products would have no expertise in the software which our company provided. This meant an opportunity for our company to merge with a larger firm looking to acquire resources which could provide additional services.

Several larger firms approached us, but one seemed to stand out for Andy and me. The reason for this was they wanted us to continue our activities and focus our time on building our brand. We thought we would be given latitude to expand our managed service offering. We could save all the expenses in building out a data center as the company that was acquiring us already had infrastructure which would support us, at least for the short-term.

This would have been the positive tipping point which we were looking for, but the economy, and other plans by the acquiring company turned it into a lifeline for survival. It would at minimum save us from a cash crunch, allowing us to meet payroll, so that we would not have to fire anyone, while giving us an opportunity to build our brand, and be rewarded with larger incentive bonuses. All of which didn't pan-out as planned.

The other tipping point in my life was the relationship I had with my spouse. The thing that accelerated the deterioration of our relationship was when Andy and I merged our two companies. This created huge resentment for her. She would constantly remind me that I should not have made Andy a 50-50 partner. First off, we were both bringing successful consulting services firms to the table, so it really was only fair for us to share in the ownership and equally split the responsibilities. The funny thing about this merger was anyone that we talked to in our business circle said the two of us were the worst fit possible and that we would never be able to survive together. To everyone's surprise we not only survived we thrived. The joint company went from about fifteen people to fifty in only a few years. We were signing more deals than ever before.

I did not understand at first why she was so upset about the merger, but part of it was pure greed. She wanted what she thought was control over the company, even though she had no official voting right in the running of the company. If I had control of the company then she could try and "manipulate" me into doing things that might have benefited her, and really were not in the best interest of the company and its employees.

During the time leading up to and just after the merger, she was convinced that I had an affair, and if that would have been bad enough, she also made up that I had a second family oversees. This landed us in marriage counseling for the next two years. I thought we were making progress, but toward the end of therapy she admitted that she still didn't believe a word I was saying. She created this scenario to get friends and family on her side and feeling sorry for her. It was painfully clear that she wanted to take it out on me for her unhappiness, she needed someone to take the fall for all of her woes.

For the last eight plus years of our marriage, we had zero physical contact. The only thing that we exchanged was a peck on the cheek come New Years Eve. No more kissing, no holding hands, no going out to dinner or the movies, nothing. In 2018 she fell and damaged her shoulder in a fall in the back yard. She used this as an excuse to move out of our bedroom and live in the guest bedroom on the first floor. She never returned to our bedroom again.

This was clearly the sign that the marriage was over. Even before this physical separation out of the bedroom, all productive verbal conversations had ended. Unless you count all the badgering and condescending comments that were part of what she would constantly utter to me or about me in front of the kids and any other family that was present at that time. There was no relationship left. Neither one of us wanted any part of the marriage, but she was in a tough place. She needed me as I was her cash machine. With out me she would have nothing.

The Economy Turned on Us

It was all going quite well, it was demanding work, with long hours. The business required most of our attention. It was working, and we were enjoying the ride. Then in 2008, the economy took a major downturn. Our business relied on companies finance and IT departments signing on for new projects and/or upgrade of their financial software, which was our specialty.

In 2008, companies were facing challenging decisions and looked to cut costs wherever possible. In the end, all new projects were put on hold or cancelled for the foreseeable future. This squeeze put us in uncharted waters. We had never laid off any of our workers since we each started our own private companies. We had recently expanded our services to include providing a SAAS model, or Software as a Service. Today, it might be considered equivalent to the applications they have in the cloud. You could look at it as one of the first subscription-based solutions that was being offered in our field. It required a substantial investment. There was no such thing as the cloud at that point. This meant making an investment into building our own infrastructure, our own data center. We were a forty plus person company at the time, but we knew we needed a serious resume from the person which was going to be running our shared services data center. So, we hired the head of the IT department for the Joints Chief of Staff of the United States government. He was a critical hire that we needed to invest in or the investment in our Software-As-A-Service offering would have been wasted.

It was a decision which we all know, having knowledge of what the cloud provides for us in today's world, was the right direction to point the company in. We just needed time to develop and expand the solution and continue to sign early adopters that could be key advocates for our solutions. Both of which we ran out of when we got to 2008. We had over a million dollars tied up in building our data center.

Now maybe a little bit of our decision was based on fear, maybe some of it was reality hitting us in the face. We never wanted to be in a position where we needed to lay people off, and until this point, we never had to. The severity and impact of the 2008 financial crisis caught everyone off guard. Cash Flow became the focus of most companies as there was no end in sight. Companies also made tough calls in having to scale back their work forces.

My partner and I knew that we had to start thinking about selling the company, while it was still an attractive asset to other companies. That is if we wanted to pull money off the table and reward our efforts for the past ten years of sacrifices. We didn't want to lose everything we worked so hard to obtain. The reality of going bankrupt was real, banks were no longer providing bridge loans to hold over companies through dark times like this.

Andy and I could not afford losing our entire company and being out of a job on top of that. Just on the horizon was my daughter going to college. In the end she was accepted by Boston University School of Arts, majoring in scenic design. Once again, the stress and anxiety were beginning to build inside me. The pressure was intensified knowing that we had little savings for any of the kid's college. Our oldest was two years ahead of her and was going to be entering college the next year with a focus on engineering. There is no denying the enormous financial burden that college put on families especially when they have multiple children attending college at the same time.

Trying to figure out how I was going to come up with those enormous tuition checks every semester generated a pressure cooker inside me that was just looking to explode. When I think back to that time I realize now that my spouse and I never planned for our kids' education, which is neglectful on our part. I guess she assumed I would do whatever it took to come up with the money and I just figured I could. However, these times were much tougher, Andy & I had to defer taking our own bonus check, as the obligations of meeting our payroll was in jeopardy.

Added to this stress was the constant reminder from my spouse of how much the house needed work, and that we needed a new kitchen, our daughter's room was too small, the air conditioning was under sized, and the list went on and on and on. The laundry list of must haves felt like it was increasing daily. It was a nonstop barrage of reminders and demands. Yet again, there was never any concern over my mental or physical health, both of which were both quickly deteriorating.

When I heard the cost estimates for the house repairs exceeding the costs of my son and daughters' four-year education, I was not only sick to my stomach, but my head was spinning out of control, trying to think of a solution which would satisfy everyone. As a sole provider for my family that was the burden that I had to live with daily, only in the hope that someone, anyone would care enough to help me out.

Finding a Way Out

When it was obvious that the economic downturn was more of a global crisis, companies were positioning themselves to be able to take advantage of when the crisis would start to ease. Deals were being made, companies' merger, or acquired the talent and technology that would strengthen their own balance sheet and increase their pipeline for potentially new work when financial pressures eased. Companies were buying others on the cheap, and an opportunity presented itself which would allow Andy and I to take money off the table while continuing to build our brand. At least that is what we were led to believe.

In our minds selling the company would be more like an extension of our business. It would provide us the cash flow which was much needed and a strong support network for our new shared services offerings. It would mean being able to retain most of our employees, with minor salary reductions. Again, at least this is what we thought, based on what they told us.

From a personal perspective this deal looked like something which could really reward me for all my hard work and sacrifices I made over the years. It would also solve my immediate financial needs and provide a structure for a strong future financial position once the world got through financial crisis. Things were taking shape, and it appeared that this was the right move to make at the appropriate time.

As we got closer to the deal signing there were things which the acquiring firm brought up, that we had to agree on, or they would walk away from the deal. They knew we wanted to sell, they had a feeling we had to sell, at least at that time we might have thought that as well. A perfect storm in which to take advantage of us. As they say, "cash is king," especially in a global economic downturn. They had the cash, and we didn't, plain and simple.

We made the best business deal that we could, based on what was communicated to us. This became a bone of contention between my wife, at the time, and myself. In her "expert" opinion, this was a horrible deal. But what no one knew except for Andy & me is that if we didn't make that deal we could have lost everything. As the divorce proceedings were getting started and I was still living in our CT house, my oldest threw out some comments to the degree that I also made a horrible deal in selling the company. I don't know how he could have any firsthand knowledge of this, because he was only about fifteen at the time the sale went down. For that matter neither did my ex.

Andy and I were the only ones which knew about any of the particulars that made up the deal. Why am I so certain about this little fact, it's because Andy and I were the only ones in the room at the time of negotiations. The deal was close to collapsing, but in the end, we managed to get the deal done and put some dollars in our pocket. This should have been enough to straighten all our finances out and make sure that we would have money for our third child's college, and all those house renovations. There were a lot of contingency clauses, and limits which had to be reached before bonuses would be awarded. Our salaries were also not guaranteed. That was one of their stipulations that they wouldn't budge on. Andy and I had a bunch of company expenses which the new company disallowed for reimbursement. Then there was Uncle Sam who wanted his 30%, and the final big expense was the promise we made to our employees; that we would share 15% of the net proceeds with all of them, based on a formula around years of service with us. I happy that they were excited about it. We were proud to give it to them, they stood by us, and they worked hard for us. My spouse resented that. She was expecting to receive the kind of money on which you could retire. Heck, I was only 46-years old. It would take a lot more than what we got, to be able to retire. Reality check: it was nowhere close to that kind of money.

The fact was that even after the reductions against the sale price, the taxes, and the employee bonuses, we both still had a job with the new company, and they were going to let us still build our brand. One reason we picked them, was because Andy and I wanted out of the administration game and wanted to spend more time developing and collaborating with our customers. We wanted to continue to build our dream. Our real payoff was to come if/when we hit our revenue targets for expanding our Managed Services offering. If we were able to build our brand, there were millions to be had. However, now looking back, I am not sure they were ever going to allow that to happen. I have no idea it would have been a win-win, all the way around.

Even though our deal did not pan out the way we had hoped, it still afforded us some cash to move our lives forward. For a brief period, I felt rather good about myself. I made a deal which should have taken care of my children's college cost, would allow me to get the house renovated, and finally have a rainy-day fund. This would give me some breathing room and peace of mind knowing that even if there were some cloudy days we would still be in decent shape.

I was also proud of the how we compensated our employees. We knew that to keep exceptional talent you had to treat them like exceptional talent. For a fifty-person firm, we paid competitive salaries. We then added a more then generous bonus plan that would compensate them for every billable hour that they worked at a client. This created a total compensation package well above the industry average.

We also made a commitment to every employee that if we were to ever sell the company and they were still employed with us, that they would proportionately share in splitting 15% of the proceeds from the sale of the company. An agreement which we honored and one that I am still extremely proud of today. In my eyes it rewarded our employees for their loyalty to us and our company. It created a structure of family belonging. This would help them to hit their own personal financial goals. A commitment which I took very seriously. This approach resulted in an exceptionally low turnover ratio. My partner and I always put the company and our employees ahead of our own personal gain.

However, the ink was barely dry on our contracts when things started changing for me and my partner. The fine print was brought to light, and the honeymoon as we understood it was clearly over. We felt more like the runt of the litter. Within in the first few weeks, all uncollected delinquent receivables were taken out of our total compensation. My salary was reduced by more than 30% in just the first six months of the acquisition. The firm blamed the economic downturn. They released any of our devoted employees which were not actively on an engagement. If we could not find them a new client after two week, they too were released. By the end of the first year only 15-of-52 employees were left employed by the firm which acquired us. This eliminated any chance of achieving our performance revenue targets, which eliminated any possibility of me getting any bonus.

By the end of the first year my total compensation compared to what it was pre-acquisition, was reduced by two-thirds. At this point why not just walk away? Maybe get a job with another company? Well, a non-compete clause, that would have required lawyers to get involved, precluded me from leaving and doing similar work for another consulting firm. Nor could I just go out and work for myself again, for a period of 18-months. The bills kept coming, once again exceeding my take home pay. My anxiety & stress levels were back and worse than before. The rainy-day fund was being drained every week. The problem was this time there would be no secondary bonus to save the day.

Instead of coming home to a welcoming, relaxing environment, an environment where I could forget the insanity of the day, I walked into a battle zone of resentment. I was greeted with conversations about the bills and attacked with questions like "so what are you going to do about all of this?," or "you said this was a good deal?," then after a bit of time came, "where did all of the money from the sale go" and "this was a horrible deal." When I thought I could not sink any further into depression, this took me to new lows. At this point in time, it would be another four years before I was diagnosed with Bi-Polar Disorder and ADHD.

My Back Against the Wall

Locked into an employment contract, no longer having my own company, and saddled with ever increasingly large consumer debt, I had no place to turn, no one to help me through these tough times. This put me in a state of panic and despair, I needed to try something, anything.

At this time, I was working a project in the United Kingdom. My stress and anxiety weighing heavy on me, I did not hesitate to visit the local watering hole that was just down the street from the hotel. Not feeling like working past 5pm, I found myself hanging out with other consultants and some of the employees of my customer. Not knowing this group of people all that well, it was a welcome distraction that no one was judging me or reminding me of all the things they thought I was doing wrong, like my spouse would be doing if I were back home in Connecticut. After a while I got to come to know the other consultants a little more and discovered they might be inclined to send some side consulting work my way if I were able to handle the workload. However, taking that work directly would be a violation of my employment contract.

I felt that this might offer some financial relief. I could not just sit back and watch my life unravel. Even though I was married, I felt so alone. I had to figure out a way to generate additional cash. I needed to figure out some kind of solution where I could take on additional work of my own without violating me employment contract and without my new employer knowing about it.

I had created companies from nothing before, so I was confident that I might be able to figure out a solution where I could still take on new work on my own without violating my employment contract. If I could find an additional resource or two that were willing to take a chance on a new venture, then just maybe, I could manage one or two contracts. That would bring in enough to fill the gap that my new employer had created.

The nature of my job was training others with the knowledge to take what I built for them and be able to maintain it in the future. In the early days of having my own company, I trained a friend of mine, a professional plumber at the time, and had him consulting on a project in less than four weeks. I got it in my head that I could do it again. I just needed a start, a side project and someone to do most of the leg work. Just enough to get me through the next six to nine months. If I could make it that long, then I would be free to pursue any new opportunities without anyone coming after me for violating anything written in the purchase agreement.

I drew up an employment contract, met with the accounting firm located in Eastern Europe. I purchased some equipment, laptop, and printer. I started training sessions with a woman who was willing to take a chance on a new venture. She had minimal experience in our technology but seemed open to spending the extra hours necessary in learning what was needed to be successful in this field. I felt sorry for this woman and wanted to help someone else, even though I could not help myself. I was thinking in the end it would work in my favor.

In the weeks that followed we would talk almost every day. There was a seven-hour time difference which required me to start my day quite a bit earlier than usual. Though it did work in my favor as I could conduct training outside of my normal working hours, so that it would not interfere with the UK project that I was working on.

As we got to know each other better our conversations crossed into our personal lives and about how one day things look great and then before you know it, you're living in the dark again. Having someone to share your problems with and not judge you in the process was a change for me. Having someone that would take the time to listen was something that no longer existed in my marriage.

Over the subsequent months I learned of this women's personal financial struggles. There were health issues in her family and housing problems hanging overhead. Knowing this and thinking about the potential deal I had on the table, I decided to provide a loan to her. This would allow her to take care of the family health issues and settle their housing problems. It was a loan, an eighty-six-thousand-dollar loan. Yes, it was a risk, but at that time I was not in a favorable position to being able to dictate terms.

After a few months it became clear that my dreaming of being about to take on side work to help my own financial situation was not working out. I did not have enough time to do the work myself, and the women that I thought could learn the technology, struggled mightily. The only thing that was left was to try and find some other way. I was able to get out of the side deal which I fought so hard to get involved with and was able to recoup about twenty-five percent of the money I loaned.

When I told my spouse about this and the money, she immediately thought I was having an affair. She could not let it go. It seemed like if she mentioned it once she mentioned it a thousand times, "nobody just gives a strange woman eighty-six thousand dollars unless you are getting something on the side in return!" Did I ever think about having an affair? Yes. Could I have taken advantage of the situation? Yes. However, I wasn't about that, it wasn't my thing. This was about getting my life and my family out of a financial disaster, not about my struggles with my marriage. The real question being, did I ever act on any of these thoughts or so-called opportunities? ABSOLUTELY NOT.

Lending her that sum of money was naive and stupid of me. I was under tremendous stress, had no one to turn to for help, and was getting tremendous pressure knowing that everyone had their hands out looking to be paid, and all of them turning to me to save the day once again. This time I had to admit failure, my Hail-Mary pass dropped untouched to the ground. I was blind to the fact that no plan at that time would have worked unless my spouse was willing to go back to work, which she was not.

From that moment in time until even today, after our divorce has been final for almost a year, she was still accusing me of an affair, still trying to get me to admit to something that never happened. I was not about to confess to something that wasn't true. I answered any and every one of her questions that she had about the situation and about everything else under the sun during our time before we started the divorce. Even though my answers were the same every time, she was never able to come to grips that I was telling her the truth. Instead of coming to grips with that, she made up her own story which she told everyone, including my kids. If you ask me, it was a cowardly thing to do.

There were other people that bought into her story especially after my ex, made up this elaborate story of me buying a house in Romania. She convinced my children that I had a second family there. What kind of mother would do something so evil, spiteful, and malicious, to her own children just for the end game of ruining my relationship that I had with the three of them. It was the perfect opportunity to sell the deadbeat dad story to everyone. You may be asking yourself why she would do this. First off there was a huge financial gain waiting for her if she could convince the mediator, and second, she is a very vengeful person. She wanted to ruin me, take away all means of me being able to have a life. She couldn't stand the thought of me being able to move on with my life without her. In the end the judge did believe the stories and awarded her an additional eighty-six thousand dollars as part of the settlement.

These lies, and elaborate stories helped her alienate my children away from me, and scored her substantial monetary gains in the process, sounds like a considerable motive to slander me. Yet, no one questioned her to provide any proof of any of her claims. To this day, this is the one thing that I wish I could have done differently. If I would have chosen the more costly direction of having a full trial, then my lawyers would have been able to ask her that one vital question...... "Do you have any proof to support any of your accusations?" That would have toppled her house of cards, because there was no proof to be disclosed.

Her intention was to try and ruin my life. Rob my children away from me, cripple me financially so that I would be so deep in debt that I could never recover. Well, I will tell you that she got close to getting what she wanted. But my life is not ruined, I was able to climb my way out of debt. The only thing she did succeed at was damaging our children psychologically. She sold them these stories and they believed her. They never question, not even once, any of the ridiculous so-called facts. They never once came to me, ever asked me what really happened.

I have the faith to believe that one day people will realize what I had to live through, and then realize the damage that she did to me was far more damaging than any financial difficulties that she had to live with. One day the truth will come out. I can stand tall behind everything I did for my family; I doubt she can do the same because of what she did to our children.

"We Don't Run!"

Take a look around you, yeah, the sky is falling
Sinners say your prayers this train is off the tracks
Nothing is forever when tomorrow's calling
Dancing with the devil take it one day back

I'm not afraid of burning bridges
'Cause I know they're gonna light my way
Like a phoenix, from the ashes
Welcome to the future, it's a new day

We don't run
I'm standing my ground
We don't run
And we don't back down
There's fire in the sky
There's thunder on the mountain
Bless this shield and this dirt I was born in (run)
We don't run

We Don't Run
Bon Jovi

Conclusion / Lessons Learned

- If you start to see negative tendencies popping, you need to address them immediately. Have a conversation with your spouse, and even your children. Your children need constant reminder of how much you love them.

- Not addressing issues as they happen will increase your anxiety. It will also not help you get any closer to a resolution. How can you expect things to get resolved if you don't communicate your feelings. Only then will you be able to determine if there is anything left in the marriage. That is of course, if you even want to repair the relationship. In my situation, my marriage needed to be repaired or ended a decade prior, but I never spoke up.

- Intimacy is a two-way street, it's a partnership. If only one of you is trying to improve it, they will be wasting their time. If you care about improving your relationship you must be willing to invest the time into it, if you don't, then don't waste your energy. Do the stand-up thing and try have a civil conversation with your spouse about going your separate ways. Things get much more complicated if you have children and if your children are minors.

- If the two of you agree to move in different directions and you have children, no matter what the age, you will be splitting as a couple, but it's imperative that you move forward together, as parents. You are doing an injustice to your children if you don't. Remember, your children need both of their parents.

- Don't be ashamed or even afraid to seek out a professional advisor. One thing they will be able to provide, among other things, are ways that you can stay focused during this process and ways to deal with the highs and lows during each stage of the proceedings. I know it helped me.

Chapter-V: Living with a Mental Disorder

You may be asking, why am I discussing the fact that I was diagnosed with having multiple mental disorders at the age of fifty. I'm not trying to hide anything, nor am I ashamed of it in any way. It answered so many questions that I had about why I struggled so much in my youth, and later in a large majority of my adult life. It caused me heightened levels of stress and anxiety in my life, during my marriage, and contributing to my inevitable divorce. However, strangely enough and in a weird way, having ADHD contributed to factors which allowed me to cope with the challenges of building my own company and being highly successful at being about to juggle multiple projects at one time.

There are hundreds of types of what has been categorized as mental disorders. Millions of people suffer from one form or another. Due to the media, and famous people coming out to support mental health and wellness it is finally getting the attention that it deserves.

For the longest time, going back decades, the doctors & scientists worked behind closed doors studying people that they categorized as being "different". People that demonstrated difficulties in coping with everyday life. What was the expert's solution? Surprisingly all the way until the 1970's the solution the doctors came up with was to remove them from society altogether. Put them in a 'mental facility,' locked them behind bars, then they told their families and loved ones that it was better for them. They drugged them, so they would be no trouble and then threw away the key. It is insane that society tolerated that kind of "medical diagnosis." In fact, if anyone deserved to be jailed it was the doctors themselves that came up with this so-called type of "treatment." Many of these people never did anything wrong. They were guilty of being different.

Many of the greatest minds of our time suffered from at least one mental disorder. Imagine where the world would be if they would have locked up Albert Einstein, Abraham Lincoln, and Winston Churchhill?

Why am I talking about Mental Disorders? Having a mental disorder can mean many things to different people. There is no disputing that people struggling with a mental disorder are not the only ones who are struggling. Friends, loved ones, and coworkers, anyone that has interactions with people with these disorders are impacted. You may be the person who feels a little "off" or you may know someone who displays some of the symptoms. The fact remains that understanding what other people are going through allows everyone to communicate better and be able to work together in dealing with these difficult situations. Everyone has issues in life, which is what makes us human beings, taking the time to understand each other, and helping each other is the only solution that makes sense.

Walking Through Life with Blinders On

Looking back, I have all these things running through my brain, and not understanding why I was the way that I was. When things went sideways, I was unable to cope with it all. Why at times could I have incredible focus, and then all of a sudden I would lose interest, lose focus, and not complete what I worked so hard to "almost" complete.

Throughout my school years I was quiet the introverted type, I was small for my age. In the third grade I was the second smallest in my grade and that included all the girls. I was afraid to stand out, afraid to engage with my classmates. Part of this was due to a speech issue that I had. Combine these and it resulted in my lack of friends throughout grade school. During my time in grades 9-12, I tried my best to avoid most of the other kids. After gym class, I never showered. I often ate lunch in a remote stairway or just outside one of the side exit doors. I knew that was not as outgoing as most of the other kids, and it scared me, as I knew there was also more to it than that. I didn't really understand it, and I guess I figured there wasn't much I could do about it. I was constantly missing the school bus, and most of my first period class on a regular basis. It got so bad that at one point the principal called my parents into the school to notify them that I would most likely not be graduating with the rest of my senior class, unless I straightened out, and started getting to school on time. My dad was in shock as never knew that I had been late to that extent. I managed to stay focused long enough to make the bus after that. I did graduate with the rest of my class come that May.

That summer, while building my landscaping business, my dad came to me to have that talk. No, it wasn't the sex talk, we never did have that talk. He talked about how he believed in me and how I could do whatever I set out to do. He talked about his first two years at college and how he completed them with a perfect 4.0 GPA. I took that as a personal challenge, so I told him if he could do it then so could I. After my first two years I was able to achieve the same perfect 4.0 GPA average. I'm surprised I was able to maintain focus for long. But once that second year was complete, I simply got bored. I proved to myself that I accomplished what I set out to do and then lost interest. The remaining two years, I barely showed up to class and squeaked out just enough to get my Bachelor of Science degree.

This pattern of success, intertwined with periods of distraction, boredom, frustration, and loneliness continued to torment me for the next twenty-five years. When you sit down for a minute to really think about that, twenty-five years of inner struggle. People talk about having "peace of mind," It took me just about half a century to really understand what people were talking about. Being able to sit with a cup of coffee in the morning and watch the sun rise, enjoying its beauty, without feeling the anxiety of having to run and take care of something. It was an amazing feeling. I've learned to cherish life, enjoy God's gifts, and now I can allow that to happen. I no longer have the anxiety which at one time imprisoned me.

What Makes Us the Way We Are

To help understand the degrees of mental health, we must be willing to investigate our lives from the beginning. We sometimes forget that it all starts with our DNA. Much of who we are, who we will become, is because of this combination from both of our parents. Who we are, is based on what we are made of. Our DNA brings the past of our parents, and their parents, and their parents into our present. This only stands to reason that to understand who we are and why we are the way we are we need to examine the past. We must investigate our family history. We need to be able to recognize the signs so that we can be able to help ourselves.

If you have questions about your life, questions about why things get you upset, why you have trouble concentrating, amongst other things, then you need to be honest and open with yourself and want to improve your life. Understanding the past is a good place to start.

My grandparents were both alcoholics and chain smokers. Quite the addictive personalities. After sixty years my grandfather was able to quit smoking and drinking and lived the remaining years realizing what he had missed during his life. He spent more time experiencing life. I was able to see how happy my children made him when he got to see them. My grandfather lived in Louisiana and my family lived in Connecticut made it extremely challenging to get together on any kind of regular basis. I feel guilty about that. There was genuine caring and loving from a man that I never really saw that emotion out of. He showed that within us, that with the right support system, one can improve their own life. He battled throat cancer, smoking four packs of cigarettes a day, and being a recovering alcoholic, but still managed to live till he was seventy-seven. I think he would agree that his last years were some of the best.

My dad, currently 86, a highly educated man, has never been tested, but has many of the common signs of being OCD. He has always liked things executed in an extremely specific manner, timing, and predictability. My mom, currently 85, only recently was tested and diagnosed with ADD. She hasn't been able to focus on a single conversation for as long as I was able to remember. Then there are the constant periods of extreme mood swings. The upsetting part of this is I can see that she constantly struggles with these challenges. Instead of being able to enjoy the remainder of her life.

I recognize these things now about my family only because my eyes were opened when it was explained to me by my doctors. After fifty years of living in the dark, it now makes sense and helps explain things about my youth. There is no absolute scientific link that mental disorders are hereditary, however, there is a higher probability that parents which have mental disorders will have children that also have some form of a mental disorder as well.

Making Sense of it All

Like people always say, "it's never too late." The same holds true in my case. I finally concluded that I needed to figure out the "why's" in my life. What was I afraid of, things couldn't get worse. Just after my 50th birthday, I dropped my prejudices and fears and made an appointment with a phycologist. I realized I had to find out the reasons behind the struggles which made my daily life a struggle.

In my case, I lived in confusion and uncertainty for fifty years. Fifty years of questions, fifty years of frustration, and fifty years of stress and anxiety. My stress, anxiety, and emotional unrest was all too real. It followed along with me my entire life, of course it did, it's in my DNA. Years later when I was diagnosed, and results proved I was bipolar and did have ADHD, it explained why my childhood was so much different than most of the other kids.

I went to the professionals, not even knowing anything about the process. They helped me understand that people are wired differently, and because of that we all have our issues with which we must deal. An estimated 26% of America's population suffers from a diagnosable mental disorder each year. Almost ten percent of American's will suffer from a depression classified illness (major depression, bipolar disorder, or dysthymia) With bipolar disorder affecting 2.6% of American adults. [4-1] This "wiring" gets disconnected from the parts of the brain which allows us to process events and activities that allow us to manage them in an orderly manner. However, this still didn't answer my questions, and it surely did not help me improve my life moving forward.

The doctor conducted a series of tests, physical and psychological. I was seated in the doctor's office and waited for the doctor to explain what all this testing proved. I was a bit anxious to say the least and before giving the doctor even the chance to sit down I asked him, if there was something physically wrong with me, and did I have ADHD?

After the doctor explained his analysis, I came to understand that having ADHD or not is not a black or white answer, and that nothing about a mental disorder is as simple as 1-2-3. The fact is that in many cases where an individual tests positive for a mental disorder, they test positive for multiple conditions. I was one such case. It was these that accelerated and intensified my problems with stress and anxiety well beyond what the average person must deal with.

I was relieved to hear that it wasn't my imagination. However, before I could ask what the next steps were, he replied, "but that is not the only thing that we are dealing with here. You are also Bipolar." Which at the time, meant little to me, as the only thing that I knew about Bipolar was that it was somehow tied to depression.

I'm not saying that this was the reason for my divorce, but I do know that it did have a serious impact not only on my marriage, my family and my entire life up to that point. I think it's important for everyone to be more aware of mental disorders and their impact on the people that suffer from them and their family and friends.

Understanding mental disorders and how it can affect people may allow you to have a better relationship with a person that may have one. You may even be able to communicate at a more effective level then before you knew the challenges that the person was facing.

One example is someone who is OCD, or obsessive compulsive disorder. This is a person who very much needs things organized in a neat and orderly fashion. By knowing this about a person you can assist them by respecting that view of the world. Maybe you are working on a project with this person, and you are not so neat and orderly. For the sake of the project and the good of the working relationship would it hurt in this case to try and be more organized and attentive? It can only improve your efficiency with future projects that you work on.

While sitting with my doctor, he explained the approach which would be taken, in determining which medications would work the best for me. The doctor discussed the process, that they would first try the combination which works for the most patients, and then it is trial & error from there. Research shows that over eighty percent of the people who have a mental disorder, struggle with multiple disorders. As a result, the solution requires what doctors call a medical cocktail. A combination of medication which would address my mood instability and my hyperactivity. They told me that it could take time to find the right combination and dosages of medication that will work with my body chemistry. In my case my body reacted favorably to the first combination of medications that the doctors recommended.

For decades people that were perceived as different, strange, or simply difficult to deal with, were sometimes called crazy. Society has a way of simply pushing aside people that appear to be different. The people who declared themselves as "normal," gave little of their time, nor patience to deal with people that just didn't "fit in" with them. This may apply to yourself, your loved ones, or even someone you just met.

Only recently have high profile stars like athletes and actors come forward to tell their stories of struggles with a particular mental illness. A struggle that has been plaguing them for most of their lives. This shift in focus has been the catalyst that the world needed so that society would sit up and listen. For the last decade society has increased its efforts to better understand and support people suffering from the many types of mental disorders that have been identified. More than ever there is a light that is shining on folks with these disorders and have showed them that they can have a better life, that things can be different.

Mental Health and Mental Disorder

I think it's important for people to understand the difference between normal mental health and mental disorders. Quite often the answer is not clear. For example, if you are afraid of giving a speech in public, does it mean you have a mental health disorder or a simple case of nerves? Or, when does shyness become a case of social phobia? Understanding how mental health conditions are identified is the first step to getting help if you feel you or someone you know falls into one, or even multiple categories.

As defined by the Mayo Clinic, Mental health is the overall wellness of how you think, feel, act, and relate to others. Mental health also affects how you feel about yourself, and how you manage the stress of everyday life. [4-2] Sometimes people experience a significant disturbance in this mental functioning. A mental disorder may be present when patterns or changes in thinking, feeling, or behaving cause distress or disrupt a person's ability to function. A mental health disorder may affect how well someone:

- Maintains personal or family relationships.

- Functions in social settings.

- Performs at work or school.

- Learns at a level expected for your age and intelligence.

- Participates in other important activities.

Even if this does not apply to you personally it's about time more people should have a better understanding of what people that do have some forms of a mental disorder are suffering through. Knowing the signs might put you in a position to better support someone who has, and you may be the catalyst for that person turning their life around.

The Diagnostic and Statistical Manual of Mental Disorders (DSM) is a guide published by the American Psychiatric Association that explains the signs and symptoms of several hundred mental health conditions, including anxiety, depression, eating disorders, post-traumatic stress disorder and schizophrenia. The DSM provides criteria for making a diagnosis based on the nature, duration and impact of signs and symptoms.

It also describes the typical course of the disorder, risk factors and common coexisting conditions.

I was shocked when I learned of these statistics for the very first time. Even though I feel into these categories, I had no idea how common place they were across the globe. I feel that the world is actually embarrassed that so many people struggle with the challenges of everyday life. Based on this data, there is a high probability that you may know someone who also struggles with a mental disorder, but you just don't recognize it.

As reported by the World Health Organization Mental Disorders: [4-3]

- In 2019; 1 in every 8 people in the world live with a mental disorder, anxiety and depression disorders being the most common.

- In 2020 alone, because of the COVID-19 pandemic, the number of people living with anxiety and/or depression disorders rose an estimated 26% and 28% respectively, in a SINGLE YEAR!

- Mental disorders involve significant disturbances in thinking, emotional regulation, or behavior. There are many are more than one hundred known mental disorders.

- Effective prevention and treatment options do exist.

- Unfortunately, many people do not have access or cannot afford effective care.

Conclusion / Lessons Learned

Living with a mental disorder is incredibly challenging and an emotional roller coaster. However, life in general is an emotional roller coaster for a lot of people without mental disorders, which masks the people that are struggling with their mental disorder makes it that much more difficult.

- If you think you have the symptoms of having some type of mental disorder, you need to get a professional opinion. It will be a huge relief one way or the other.

- If you do suffer from a mental disorder and are still struggling with getting on top of it, don't give up trying. Now more than ever society is opening up to this mental health challenge.

- Don't be embarrassed talking about it. Living in the dark and alone is far more dangerous and harmful. People will understand.

- Some of the greatest minds in history have had some form of a mental disorder and if they did not conquer their fears and turn their affliction into an advantage the world would not be the same without them.

- Understanding your strengths and weaknesses, and the environments where they exist will help you gravitate to the environments which are strengths for you and avoid the environments which expose your weaknesses. If you feel you always need to be outdoors during the day, then don't take a job as a night watchman in a factory. Focus on getting into the right field, and not necessarily chasing the highest paying job.

Section II: There's No Turning Back

When you finally come to the realization that a divorce is inevitable, it's time to prepare for the worst. You may be thinking that I'm taking this a bit too far, that I'm crazy, but as they say, "buyer beware". Divorce will probably be one of the worst thing that happens to you in your lifetime. It can ruin you financially, but even worse it could destroy the relationship you have with your family, your children. There are many aspects of a divorce that you may not experience, but why not be prepared for anything in case they do come up.

You may be thinking that if you follow all the rules, agree to what's put on the table, then things will be wrapped up before you know it. You think you will save money in the process and be done with your spouse forever. Think Again. Regardless of what you think you know, it's not enough to get you all the way to the end. The more your spouse wants to battle you, the longer and more difficult getting this done will be.

Communication is a key component in any negotiation, but in a divorce situation it can add to your detriment. In a divorce situation the appearance of communication and the assumption that it's getting you closer to a resolution can just be a tactic, a distraction used by your spouse and their lawyers. Remember, depending on the complexity of your case, you could be at war and not even know it. In my case the other side was looking to inflict as much pain and suffering on me as possible. In the beginning, I was naïve enough to think that my spouse would want a quick resolution so that she could move on with her life, she was doing quite the opposite. She was in the mist of directing a theatrical production with me as the central character, a smear campaign, intended to annihilate me as the end goal. Do not confuse communication with manipulation.

My advice, work everything through your lawyer. Stay as far away from your spouse as possible. You don't want anything you may regret later. Just like in war, the other side is trying to confuse you, distract you, trick you into giving them information that they can turn around and use against you. It will be much less stressful on you if you can minimize the senseless back and forth banter between you and your spouse. The goal has always been or should always be to end your marriage and move on with the rest of your life. Nothing more.

Know it or not, depending on the specifics of your situation, and how much your spouse wants this divorce to happen or not, you will be in for a lifetime worth of arguments, accusations, and manipulation. It may not appear this way in the beginning, but your spouse is out for themself and cares little for your health and well-being. Unless you count burying you in a mound of debt and driving a stake between you and your children as my spouse did to me.

If you have been the sole or majority income provider, you have been providing for everything that your family has and is accustomed to spending. At one point during this process, it will dawn on your spouse that their life is going to drastically change, and they are not going to be happy about it. Many times, greed and fear will overcome them which is an ugly combination, believe me I've seen it. There will be a lot of folks, people that you once considered friends and even family that will turn against you. Keep your focus on the end game. Before you know it, all of the ugliness will be behind you.

Chapter-VI: Finding a Good Lawyer

To this point I've been talking about things revolving around you and your spouse. However, the most important part of the entire process, the most important action you will take, is finding a good lawyer which you are comfortable with. It's not just a good lawyer that is required, it's one that you are comfortable working with that will make the difference.

Most of what we think we know about divorce lawyers is from what we watch on TV. For me it was Arnie Becker, where Corbin Bernsen, played a goofy lawyer who most of the time was trying to get involved with his female clients. We see that many of the lawyers treat you as just another client and that only a rare few really cared about you as a person. However, we all know that this is no TV show, and there is no guarantee around the outcome of your case.

When all the dust settles, a large part of your case, and what you will be responsible for when it's all over will be left in the hands of a complete stranger. A person that you know little to nothing about. A person that for the next three to six months, or even one to two years, will represent you in front of the eyes of the court. It will be up to your lawyer to orchestrate the telling of your side of the story so that you walk away from this marriage with an arrangement that you can live with. An arrangement that lands somewhere in the middle of what each party is asking for would be preferrable.

If you have minor children, under the age of eighteen, the fate of how often, when, and where you and your children will live, falls in the balance.

First Impressions

Having the right lawyer is easily the most crucial step in getting you out of your marriage. If you're not comfortable with lawyer(s) or something about the firm in general bothers you, then move on to finding another lawyer. You are going to spend a lot of time with this person, e-mails, calls, texts, occasional face-to-face sessions, so you need to be comfortable with the law firm and the lawyer who is going to represent you.

Don't just jump onto the internet and do a search for "divorce lawyers"! Given the society we are living in, I'm sure you know at least one or two friends/family/coworkers who have been involved in or know someone who has gotten divorced. Gaining information of the firm and person that will be representing you is a critical part of the evaluation process. The next check point will be to meet this person and to see if the two of you have chemistry with one another.

In my case, when I told a friend of mine, that my marriage had not been going well for years and that I realized it was over, he suggested a lawyer that his brother used to represent him in his divorce. He mentioned the lawyer, Janis, that his brother used felt comfortable working with her, and happy with the settlement arrangement.

I set up the appointment with Janis's assistant. When I showed up at her office, I liked what I saw. It was a quiet little law firm, in a quaint little house. Not knowing what to expect, I knew I wanted a lawyer that would handle the case herself and not dish off to some young less experienced junior lawyer.

When Janis came into the room, I immediately had a calm confident feeling about her. I tend to talk a lot, and I do a lot of talking with my hands, yes, I'm Italian. She "got me" right out of the gate. We sat down at the table, Janis sat across from me. She wasted no time and got right into it. I liked that she pulled no punches. "There is nothing I hate more than a liar! You tell me the truth about everything I ask, or this is not going to work!" Janis was firm but respectful. I liked her right away. She wasted no time educating me on how all this divorce stuff works. Five minutes into the conversation I knew that I found the person that I wanted to represent me.

Your Life is in your Lawyer's Hands

Your lawyer is a direct link to the outcome of your case. You need to have a personal bond with your lawyer, you must feel at ease and comfortable talking to your lawyer about anything that has happened during the life of your marriage. This is the person who will be defending you, pleading your case, covering your back when you're not around, or not allowed to speak for yourself. It's something not to take lightly. Just like no two people are alike, no two lawyers are alike either. Remember the outcome of these proceedings will dictate how you are going to live your life.

A few key points:

- Tell your lawyer EVERYTHING. Do not hold anything back. There may be things that you think are unimportant, but let your lawyer make that decision. Good or bad, get everything out in the open, lawyers hate surprises. The other side is going to dig into your life and believe me they will find out if you are trying to hide something. Giving the other side ammunition is the last thing you want to start doing.

- If you did do something in your past that you are not proud of, or are ashamed of, your lawyer needs to know about it. What you don't tell your lawyer could come back to hurt you. No one likes to be blind-sided, especially lawyers. If your lawyers know as much of your life as possible the better, they can deal with it. Let them decide if something is relevant to your case or not.

- Please don't insult them by thinking you are smarter than they are, it's embarrassing. You may know a little about areas of the law, but you are still an amateur, and they do this for a living. This is your first "case," and hopefully your last, your lawyer has done hundreds. If you don't explicitly trust your lawyer, get another lawyer.

- Ask questions, ask a lot of questions. This will not only help you, but it will help bring to light particulars of the case that might not have come up in casual conversation. The questions you ask can sometimes provide your lawyer with insights that they find particularly useful.

- Keep an open dialog with your lawyer. You want to keep in step with everything that is happening. Be very responsive to your lawyer's requests. The longer you go dark, could give the impression that the other sides argument has merit. Provide as much information and context as possible, in a timely fashion.

- Forget about the cost. The cost of their services is about the time your case will require and how long it will take to settle. What venue will be used to argue the merits of you case? Will it be a full trial? Will depositions be required? Will you go to mediation instead of an expensive trial? The cost will be impacted by issues, items that your spouse is going to bring up. Every time your spouse states an accusation, it will be your lawyer's responsibility to reply to it. In today's court system, the father is guilty until he proves himself innocent. The cost is going to be the costs. Know this going in. Trying to take short cuts or trying to minimize the time just to save a couple of bucks will cost you much more in the long run.

Conclusion / Lessons Learned

Once you realize there is no option for reconciliation, you should be realizing that a huge burden in your life will be lifted, then it's time to get started. The following will be the most important decisions you will make over the length of your divorce proceedings:

- Do not rush into selecting a lawyer.

- Find a friend, family member or coworker who has had a good experience with a reputable lawyer.

- First impressions are everything. If it does not feel right, then continue your search.

- Be honest and open with your lawyer, every step of the process.

- Be responsive to your lawyer's needs and requests for information. Remember even the smallest "nothing's" could mean something from a professional legal perspective. Your future is in the hands of your lawyer, help them be successful.

Chapter-VII: She Said! – He Said!

In what is supposed to be a fair and just due process of the law, quite often comes down to the positioning by the lawyers and probability, instead of being about finding out the truth.

I didn't say that it was fair. I know it was not fair in my situation. I am hoping that nothing like what happened to me is used against you like it was me. In my case, pieces of the facts were used to get it to appear that the fabricated accusations would also be true, by association. You may not even get wind of the made up stories and lies that were told about you until after the settlement terms have been determined.

There are two sides to every story and in my case, I was guilty of finding someone that I could tell my side of the story who did not have any bias or prejudices. I am guilty of having conversations with people that I met on Facebook. Did I ever meet these people in person, of course not. They were from different walks of life from different areas of the country, and some from different countries altogether.

My spouse would like everyone to believe that I had all of these romantic rendezvous in the middle of the night in exotic places like Hong Kong, but these were all made up fantasies created to paint the worst picture of me as possible. She even told these stories to our children. These conversations took place during some of the most heated controversies of the divorce proceedings. While I am sure she had her fan club to support her all along the way, I pretty much had no one in my corner. Remember I still needed to put in long working hours in order to continue making payments on all of the bills. Leaving little time for me to unwind. I basically got off work and went right to sleep.

Once it gets into this stage of lies and accusations, having proof, is the only way to really settle these disagreements. In my case I had the proof exonerating myself, but no one cared to listen, and no one questioned her on being able to actually be able to prove her stories were real. She never provided any material support which backed up her claims. I lost track at how many times I was told by my lawyer how she continually brought up things that in the end I could disprove. Somehow though she still got everything she was crying over and then some.

She was nowhere close to the women that I fell in love with some thirty years ago. It was towards the end of the proceedings where I cut off all ties, ignored all her rantings and accusations. It didn't matter anymore that it probably cost me more money. I just had to get away from all her greed and negativity. I moved out at the end of January, 2022, and the divorce was not finalized until July.

Twisting the Truth

In my case, my spouse took a few facts, not necessarily pertaining to me, joined them together and created what some believed to be a plausible story, that I had something to hide. She created a world that never existed, a dream state where I was the evil emperor with wives all around the world. Well, that guy never existed. Yet I was the one that had to pay the price.

One such example was where my spouse used a new Verizon phone number to claim it was some kind of secret burner phone which I had purchased to keep in contact with a secret romance I was having in Hong Kong! When in fact that new Verizon phone number was the inventory number that they assigned to my spouses Apple-watch that our daughter got her for Christmas. The sad part about all of this is that everyone believed her. Discounting the fact that all she had was a phone bill with a phone number on it, when it was her dang Apple watch!

To clear my name, I had to spend hours with the reps from Verizon who then went through our account. In the end this mysterious phone number was assigned to my spouses Apple watch that she activated just a few months prior. It took about an hour to track through every device on our account and which device belonged to which number. Unfortunately, I'm pretty sure that her lawyers were the only ones that heard the truth be told!

During my quest for the truth, Verizon let me in on their own procedures and inventory tracking system. To track for billing purposes, every device that a person has, Verizon assigns each device with a ten-digit number so that each device can be charged according to the particular contract. It appears on the bill as a phone number, even though it may not be an actual phone. This is the only way that they can properly track that inventory for invoicing purposes. The reason this number was not familiar to my ex was because she never bothered to go to the Verizon story to get the truth about the mysterious phone.

The facts were irrelevant to her. In fact, they disproved her accusations, so it was best she just not bring them up at all. She had what she wanted, a small piece of a single fact, that she then spun into an elaborate fantasy. The truth, that this "phone" was not a physical phone at all, but an Apple-watch synced to her Apple phone, was something my kids were never told about. In fact, I doubt anyone, but her lawyers ever knew about the truth. Want more proof? I have only ever been an Android owner, so I have never owned an I-watch, or any other Apple device.

To the average person this story might have seemed plausible, but these were the same people who wanted to see me punished for what they think I did. They wanted me punished because now my spouse would have to fend for herself. Her closest family members and even our children had no clue as to the lavish spending habits that she had, and the demands that she put upon me. No one ever knew, or for that matter could ever imagine the kind of debt we were in. Even when I was able to substantiate my findings with bank and financial records, I was accused of making them all up on the computer.

People want someone to blame when they start hearing stories. It doesn't matter if the facts didn't support these stories. They needed someone to blame for everything that went wrong in their own lives. When the facts contradicted their accusations, they conveniently bury them. Then they fill the gaps with fairy tales that seem plausible to the average listener. These fairy tales appeared to be real and they funneled all of the blame down to me. I was the patsy that was going to take all the heat. I could see them sitting around the kitchen table drinking their favorite alcoholic beverage, as they so often did, just laughing about how they stuck it to me. Me ex being proud of the job she did in slandering me, and in the process getting everything she wanted.

In my case, her friends and family, our own children, and most importantly the court system made up their minds long before the truth could be told. In fact, I did not even get a chance to tell what really happened in most of the cases. Heck, it took writing this book to be able to tell my side of the story. I'm hoping that word gets back to them all. My kids deserve to know the truth about what I did and did not do. They need to hear the truth about the accusations which their mother made up. The facts are that there was no secret burner phone, there was no affairs, no second family, no thousands of dollars hidden in the walls, or buried in the backyard, nor any Swiss bank accounts. This is not the movies, it was an story of two people who grew apart and, in the end, got a divorce.

What Really Happened

Being able to tell someone else my story, and my frustrations and loneliness I was experiencing was nice to get off my chest. It was a welcome change to be able to share my side of the story, my problems with someone that would listen. Talking through some of the things that were overwhelming me made it a little more palatable. God knows that for the last eight years of our marriage my spouse was never there for me, mentally nor physically. I will say she was always right there to correct me, ridicule me and continually barrage me with condescending verbal attacks. She never missed an opportunity to try and knock me down.

Yet again, a small fact was spun into an elaborate fantasy. A single fact that I was having conversations with an Asian woman, was then twisted into an elaborate plan to paint me as unfaithful husband and a deadbeat father. My spouse convinced people, and our children that I had a second family in Hong Kong, and they were just waiting to be reunited with me. The simple fact is I have never been anywhere in Asia or near Asia, nor did I ever have a face-to-face meeting with this mysterious Asian woman. These undeniable facts make it impossible to have done what she convinced people that I did. The really sad part is that no one, not even my own children questioned her to prove that anything other than conversations ever happened. She never had to prove any of these facts to collaborate her story. She was probably proud of the fact that she was ripping apart the relationship her children had with their father, filling their emotions with hatred and anger towards me. I guess, that was her plan all along. I forgot the part where she gets rich in the process. My whole life was my kids, and she made clear that her life was all about greed, deception, and vengeance. She got her way; our settlement left me penniless and with six figures in debt, and kids that no longer wanted any part of their father in their lives.

My three children are the loves of my life, my reason for living, and my purpose in life. How could any parent use their own children as pawns in some kind of sick game that they were playing to brain wash them against their father. Hearing the outlandish lies that their own father had a second family in another country must have been devastating to them. It conjured up feelings of rage and hostility that were unfounded.

Who does that to their own children. My spouse didn't care about the permanent damage she was inflicting on her own children, as long as I was the one that was getting punished. As long as she was able to drive a stake between her children and their father, keeping them close to her so that they would never leave her side, then it was all justified in her eyes.

I hope that after finding out about this book from friends or family she will paint the pitcher of me and it won't be of a man beaten down, broke and forced to live with his parents. That picture is now a work of art, and it shows how I continued on with my life, never looking back. I made new friends, I'm no longer in debt, 40 pounds less, pension fund rebuilt beyond what the courts gave her, wrecked BMW restored, good as new, sitting sipping coffee in the lanai of my three bedroom home, that I renovated myself. I'm proud of all that I have accomplished in just over two short years. But I'm even more proud that I kept my integrity and dignity over the course of the entire ordeal. I walked out of that mediation upset about the settlement, but my head held high as I was confident that nothing was going to stand in my way of rebuilding my life. Something that my ex could never claim. That is something she will have to live with. What she did to our children will follow her for the rest of her life.

Conclusion / Lessons Learned

- In most divorces there will be disagreements, of course there are, you're getting a divorce how can there not be any disagreements.

- Do not ignore, nor dismiss things that your spouse may be saying, just because you know them to be false, or they just may be recognized as the truth but people that wouldn't know any better. Like the judge, mediator, or family and friends.

- Stick to the facts. Don't get into a back and forth full of accusations and lies. When things are said that are not factual, then you must question them, ask for the other side to provide some sort of proof that their accusations are in fact warranted. This will establish a precedent for future accusations, and the need for them to prove everything that they say about you. Something that did not happen in my case.

- Refrain from making false accusations yourself. In most cases, it will only make you look worse if anyone proves you wrong. Yes, people make mistakes in their assessment of the facts, or don't know all of the facts at the time of the accusation. Do Not just make things up because they may make your case look stronger or may make your spouse look worse. Either way I recommend sticking to the truth.

Chapter-VIII: Surviving the Divorce

Plain and simple, pay attention, try to make sure you understand each of the things that will come up over the entire proceeds; no matter how insignificant it may seem. You may have to live with these things the rest of your life. If your spouse comes after you in an illogical, vengeful, or downright mean approach, resist replying right back in anger, instead have your lawyer fight your battles. Remember, no matter how tired you may be, how stressed you are, you can't ever back down, never quit!

During every step of the divorce proceedings, you must be on your guard. Your spouse could be spinning stories and creating accusations that you are not aware of, and then when you finally hear about them, they have gained traction and could be perceived as the truth, even though no evidence was presented to back up these claims. You will find yourself in the position of being guilty before the trial or mediation has ever begun.

You must be ready to react and defend your position against everything that is thrown at you. I know it will be hard but try and not take this personally. This might be exactly what the other side is hoping for. It could be a strategy to get you to overreact, blow up, or lose your cool. I know it will be hard to control yourself in the heat of the moment. I know it was for me, but you need to resist any verbal banter with your spouse. There are many other ways to fight back which will be far more effective. What worked for me is I had a vision of what my life was going to be like after the divorce dust settled. After I paid off my debts. This new life is truly a gift from God. These thoughts and hope for the future allowed me to relax and better handle all of the garbage that my ex and her lawyers were throwing at me. In the end I think it started to frustrate them more than it did me.

Stay focused and address each accusation, each lie, one at a time. Fight back with the facts and all the details. Provide your lawyer with the particulars that will be needed to prove you correct or defend the circumstances leading up to the accusations. You need to stand your ground and don't back down. The only way that you can survive this ordeal is to follow the lead and advice of your lawyer, remember even though this is your first time in the ring, it's not your lawyers.

If you are looking for a little motivation, something that slaps you in the face when you start getting distracted? Remember these words by Tom Petty.

Well, I won't back down
No I won't back down
You could stand me up at the gates of hell
But I won't back down

No I'll stand my ground
Won't be turned around
And I'll keep this world from draggin' me down
Gonna stand my ground
And I won't back down

Hey baby; There ain't no easy way out (I won't back down)
Hey I will stand my ground
And I won't back down

Well, I know what's right
I got just one life
In a world that keeps on pushin' me around
But I'll stand my ground
And I won't back down

Hey baby; There ain't no easy way out
Hey I will stand my ground (I won't back down)
And I won't back down

Hey baby
There ain't no easy way out (I won't back down)
Hey I won't back down
I won't back down

Hey baby; There ain't no easy way out (I won't back down)
Hey I will stand my ground (I won't back down)
And I won't back down (I won't back down)
No, I won't back down.

"I Won't Back Down"
Tom Petty & The Heartbreakers

You Can't Know Everything

It may seem hopeless to try and fight the tide, but if you're not prepared, it will come back to bury you. Be ready to invest a considerable amount of time to defend your position. You need to be prepared for any question and any requests for information. You need to be ready to prove that these accusations and stores are just fabrications made up by your spouse to make your spouse look like the innocent victim, and you are the deadbeat low life that is the reason their lives are turned upside down.

I won't lie to you, this is going to be a lot of work, believe me, I lived through it. I spent countless hours gathering information across 1,100 documents to generate supporting information to discredit her lies and fabrications. If you sit back and do nothing, thinking that eventually the truth will come out in the end, you are in for a rude awakening.

I feel that times have changed over the years and now you are guilty until you prove yourself innocent. My spouse made accusations against me in front of our family and friends, she painted a horrible picture of me as a husband and as a father. She used these to her advantage. All along she knew she made these things up to get what she wanted from me. Everyone hears the accusations and lies, but nobody cares about the retraction printed on some page buried in the back of the newspaper. I'm guessing that in my case, the retractions were never communicated back to anyone, especially my children. For all they knew they were all true as they never took the time to follow through and verify the facts on any of the stories. It was simple for them to turn a blind eye on the truth. It's exactly as my spouse planned it. It's one of the main reasons my children still have not spoken to me since the divorce was finalized.

Even though no one got to hear the truth, I still was able to vindicate myself by proving to everyone that my spouse fabricated a story of me cleaning out the joint bank account. I proved to her lawyers that it was in fact my spouse that was caught on Bank surveillance tapes going to the ATM machine and withdrawing all the money from our joint account. Her lawyers replied that maybe next time they should have asked her for some proof before they went off and accused me of wrong doings.

The real fact was at the specific time that the money was being withdrawn, I was on the 12th hole playing golf in, The Villages, sunny Florida, when I got a call from my lawyer asking me what was going on! Being in the state of Florida at the time was not enough to prove my own innocence. Once again it was up to me to prove my ex made up the entire story. It was up to me to find additional prove of my innocence, so I started digging.

Fortunately for we live in an age of cell phone cameras, online banking, and security surveillance. I discovered that the funds were indeed withdrawn from our own ATM branch, in Newtown Connecticut during a time that I was in Florida. Maybe I rented a private jet helicopter and flew back to Connecticut just so I could withdraw $900.00 dollars. I guess that would be silly, just like the rest of the stories she would make up. Once I found the exact date and time of the withdrawal it was easy. I went to the bank where they confirmed it was my spouse that withdrew the funds from the bank not me.

Only when we asked her lawyers if they wanted to see video footage of her withdrawing those funds herself did they back off the accusations. When confronted by her lawyers she finally admitted that she "forgot" that she was the one that made the withdrawal. It would have been prudent for her lawyers to ask their client if she had any real proof of her accusations before they accused me of the crime.

This was just one of dozens of lies and accusation my spouse made up about me. The real crime was not that she was the one that withdrew the funds, but that everyone that she told heard the accusation, and very few if any, knew that she was the one that set me up to take the fall. I'm sure she painted the picture that I was a dead-beat dad, only out to harm my children's mother, and leave her destitute with no home or money. Now that is funny!!! When in fact this was just another point in her plan to paint a picture of me that my kids could not turn away from, nor forgive their dad for. It was part of her plan to rob me of everything. I'm pretty sure she never told our children that she fabricated the entire story.

Hopefully, one day my children will be curious enough to read this book and begin to understand what really transpired those last eight years of their parent's marriage. I'm hoping that they realized their mother was lying to them, for her own benefit, for her own financial gain. She was lying to them to keep them as close to her as possible and as far away from their father.

It's Never Too Soon to Prepare

The ATM withdrawal accusation was only one of dozens of stories that were told over the course of a year, who knows how many your spouse is going to try and conjure up. That being said, my advice to you is that it's never too soon, nor too later to prepare for the possibility that your spouse is going to play these manipulative games.

You have a large task ahead of you, and to be perfectly honest, it may get worse before it gets better. You need to start preparing all the documentation and paperwork that will be requested from you. You need to make a list of the things that you think your spouse may try and spin against you. You can't anticipate all of them, but each one that you can prepare for will put you in that much better shape.

One of the most important things during these divorce proceedings is to be prepared and expect the unexpected from your spouse during the entire length of the divorce proceedings.

You will be far better off if you're prepared and not need the information than to be blind-sided by false accusations, or embellished stories, if you're not prepared.

It makes a huge difference in having the information at your fingertips when needed rather than having to try and piece together the information after the fact. I have put together a list of things to think about, or plan for, before things get too heated. It will also be valuable information for your lawyer to have.

You may already have some of these things in motion. This puts you a little ahead of the game, for the moment. It will also save you a lot of money down the road, as it will require your time and not your lawyers time to gather and categorize all the data. Use this time to keep you focused on the particulars of the case and not your emotions. They include, in no particular order:

- Having a checking account solely in your name. If you are the sole provider you will have to continue to pay all of the bills. In my case I did not have enough money as it was before the divorce. I could ill afford my bank account being cleaned out in the middle of the night. You name is on all of these bills and they will be your responsibility if you have the money or not. Having a secure bank account will guarantee that the funds will be there for when you need them.

- If you have a joint account, I advise taking half the money out and moving it to your personal account. Leaving half of the funds behind. This way you can't be accused of not being fair. It will be too late to get the money back, if your spouse decides to clean out the entire account before you know what hits you. You will have a difficult time getting that money back once it has disappeared.

- Have at least one credit card that is in your name alone. Order a free credit report, you will be asked to do this soon enough by your attorney.

- Make a list of all your assets and liabilities of which you are aware. This includes any retirement funds, insurance policies, and bank accounts. Keep an eye in the mail for all statements that will prove the existence of "hidden" accounts. Like was the case with my ex she had a secret credit card that for years I did not know she had. It was when I was gathering up all of the financial statements that I found a credit card statement for a card that I had never seen before.

- Keep a copy of every email, text message, or any other form correspondence between you and your spouse, or from any event which you think might be tried to be used against you. There will be a time when you may have to go back in time and try to recall particulars of a situation. Keeping all correspondence will give you the backup and more importantly, will preserve the real facts.

- Depending on your circumstances be prepared to supply up to five years of your family's financial information. Hopefully, you already have access to most of this information electronically. If you do not start making this request to each of the institutions that your and/or your spouse have had any transactions with. If you are unable to get access to these records online, then you will have to go on a crusade to request this information be sent to you through the mail. Think of it as a running log of all the activities from your marriage for the past five years.

- In most states the responsibility for the debts is split between both parties. In my case, since I was the sole supporter and income wage provider in the family, they deemed her unable to generate income, hence they saddled me with eighty percent of all our joint debt. Yet they decreed that she get eighty percent of the proceeds from the sale of our house and my entire pension. I'm hoping that you do not suffer anywhere near this devastating. Try and plan ahead. Have these discussions with your lawyer(s).

- You need to end as much of the financial dependency as possible. Over the coming months and maybe years, you'll need to minimize the spending damage that can be done in any of your accounts. Cancel what credit cards you can, reduce limits if you cannot cancel them. You will need any extra cash to continue to pay the family expenses and now your lawyer's fees and expenses.

Guilty until Proven Innocent

Nowadays, more times than not it is the husband who has been predetermined to be guilty of being the reason for the divorce. Or if only one of the spouses generated most or all the family finances, it is predetermined that this individual, father, or mother, is penalized for providing all that financial security. Unfortunately, quite often when it's time to tell your side of the story, they have already made up their minds so anything you say won't change their minds. Even in the eyes of our so called "unbiased" judicial system.

If you fall into one of these categories, you need to fight hard to get your side of the story heard. To do this you must bring clear proof of why in this divorce case the consensus is incorrect. Unless you have been involved in some kind of abusive situation, then why should you be the one that has to front the burden of the debt or lose custody of your children when it was both of you who created this situation. The courts are punishing you for doing the right thing, they are punishing you for putting your family first, and they are punishing you for being a good parent.

Just because you are the sole monetary provider for the family. There is something wrong with our judicial system.

It is critical that you obtain as much information that supports your case as possible. In my case that included gathering over a thousand financial documents. Accounting for every transaction that the family spent over the last five years of the marriage. With that kind of volume, you better be organized. You need to have a solid computerized inventory filing system. Having one central location for all the files you have sent your attorneys will save you time overall. Your spouse's legal team will be asked several times to produce the same documentation.

Depending on your circumstances you may find yourself battling for custody or visitation rights for your children or fighting for your financial solvency. To tip the scales in their favor your spouse might be the kind of person who will stop at nothing to get what they think they deserve while punishing you as much as possible along the way.

Your spouse's lawyer will take the information provided to them and try and paint a picture of how awful you are as a person, and how neglectful you were as a parent as well as a spouse during the marriage. Don't be looking for glowing endorsement for all the good that you provided to your spouse and your family over the years. If you were able to be the sole support of your family, it will be highlighted that you were never home for your family when they needed you and that it was your spouse that had to raise your children all alone during that time. I'm not saying that this view is unfounded, there very well may be a lot of times where your spouse must handle the parenting without you. I mean, really, you are the one that must provide for the family which entails you to be at your job. Until recently recent years, since Covid, most employees did not have the option of working from home. Making it their responsibility to be away from the family in order to provide for them.

Everything that you try to provide will be trivialized, while anything that went wrong during the marriage will be spun into terrible injustices on your part. Even when you can prove that the accusations were falsified, many of them will be quickly glazed over like if they never happened and you were somehow at fault regardless of what the facts prove.

Your lawyer will do their best, but we all know that there is little that can be done once people have made up their minds about something. There will be more times than you can count where outright lies and elaborate stories are told about you. This is yet another reason to make sure you tell your lawyer everything about yourself, your marriage, and how you treated your spouse and kids; do not hold anything back. Even if you were not the perfect parent and/or spouse. Remember it take two to make a marriage fall apart!

Don't rely on your spouse having to prove that their allegations have merit. As many folks want to make up their minds quickly, quite often they do not wait for both sides to tell their side of the story. They make their own conclusions based on what sounds reasonable, quite often not looking for any substantiation of the claims put forth.

The Battle for Custody

In my case our children were all adults at the time of our divorce, but a lot of divorces have this situation front and center in the battles they must face, before their divorce can be finalized. Fathers particularly have long odds in getting custody of their children and are even challenged with getting a fair share of time with their children.

Once again, the father is guilty and unsubstantiated claims go unchallenged. Your spouse will paint a picture of you being a bad parent, not be around for your kids when they needed you most. Others may make up lies that you were an abusive spouse and/or parent. Anything to get what they want. There is too much real abuse in this world without people trying to use others who are suffering through real life tragedy for their own personal benefit. The system is punishing the wrong people. Recently they have made this last point a crime, but that would entail the court system to actually be listening to the allegations and then holding the spouse accountable.

For generations, the father was expected to support the family financially, and the mother would spend more time raising their children. Does that make you any worse of a parent? Does having to support and protect the family make the father an unfit parent? Why then do the courts decree the mother custody of the children, and severely handcuff the father for visitation rights most of the time? I get that children under the age of eighteen need to be with their mother, but taking away most of the visitation rights of the father is punishing the children and doing irreputable damage, and not just punishing the father.

Only when the mother clearly demonstrates that she is an unfit mother will the court consider custody going to the father. Studies have documented that less than twenty-five percent of divorced fathers get to see their children more than once a week after the divorce. Are you kidding me? This is a horrific statistic. Studies conducted by Census.gov and legaljobs.io. goes into even more shocking statistics, around the effects on the children of fatherless homes.

Never Involve the Children

Experts agree, when children are exposed to the details of a divorce, their lives will be severely impacted, well beyond the duration of the divorce proceedings. If you are thinking about this tactic against your spouse, the mother or father of your children, I implore you to stop immediately. Trying to turn your own children against the other parent is cowardly, damaging, and destructive to your own children's mental health. These facts are undisputed over the scientific communities.

There is no good that will come from involving your children. In fact, it will certainly look bad on you, instead take the high road. Resist the knee jerk reaction if your spouse starts down this road. This is easier said than done, knowing that your spouse and even her lawyers are building their own plan that, might not describe you as a parent of the year candidate. You must think of your children and the future relationships you hope to have with them after the divorce is final.

Use your lawyer to communicate with your spouse's lawyers. Greed and hatred can change people, make them do things that they normally wouldn't do, but that is still no excuse. It is all an attempt to rattle you in front of others, catch you at a weak moment to damage your standing in the eyes of the courts, and anyone else who they are trying to sell their lies to.

Being kept in the dark, I did not realize the level over involvement my spouse engaged had engaged the kids with. She painting a pitcher that I was some degenerate neglectful father and husband, not worthy of a second of their time, and that I should be punished. This yet another reason for my writing this book. I hope that one day, I will be able to have some kind of relationship with my children again, before it's too late!

You and your spouse are getting a divorce not you and your children, so why involve them. You are only being selfish if you do. No good can come from it.

For God sake, please leave your kids out of the divorce details:

- If you have children under the age of eighteen, you or your spouse could be guilty of parental alienation. Unfortunately after the age of eighteen they are considered adults, and the abusive parent cannot be charged.

- A divorce is not your children's doing, nor is it their responsibility to engage or be drawn into its ugliness. In the end they could recent you for doing so.

- The more your children are drawn into the mudslinging the larger the chances for psychological problems [6-1], and the higher probability of suffering from depression, stress, and anxiety.

- The children may blame you for the dissolution of the marriage or they may recent you for the upheaval to the family.

- If you want a shoulder to cry on, turn to a friend or other family member. Depending on their age, children often have difficulty processing such emotions. It's not your child's responsibility to give comfort to you.

- Your children may grow up resenting you for sharing too much of the details. They may look back and feel that you were forcing them to help you through the divorce when they really needed you to support them.

- Children that witness their parents' hostility toward one another tend to experience depression, anxiety, obsessive worrying, difficulty concentrating, staying focused, and difficulty regulating their emotions. [6-2]

- They may also experience aggressiveness, anger, academic difficulties, poor peer relationships, resentment of authority, inability to adapt to new situations, sexual acting out, to name a few. [6-3]

- These conditions and behaviors may continue into adulthood and affect their ability to cope with difficulties as an adult. [6-4]

- Studies have also shown that observing parental conflict affects children not only in the moment but can also affect them for the rest of their lives. [6-5]

- The children may have a burning desire to punish you for involving them in the details.

- Lingering anger or resentment that the life they were accustomed to will no longer be possible.

- The person who involves the children beyond the bare minimum often wants to be the center of attention for their children. They do not want to share time with their spouse now that they will be divorced. Eventually the children will be of an age where they will realize what was done and recent the parent for being so selfish while not looking out for them, when they needed it most.

Don't hold them back for your own personal and emotional needs. Let them grow and become their own person, making their mark on the world.

Conclusion / Lessons Learned

- Never panic, keep everything in perspective. Take it one step at a time, one day at a time, and you can see it through.

- If you prepare and do your homework, you will survive. Work closely with your lawyer to identify those key issues which could sway the final agreement.

- Ask questions if you are not clear about anything your lawyer asks. Listen and learn from your lawyer.

- If you are going to get through this, you need to be able to break away. For at least thirty minutes a day you need to try and relax and recharge. To survive the long haul, your mind needs to be able to cool down. Do not neglect your mental health through all of this.

- Try and hook up with friends, family, and co-workers for a little R&R time, catch up on the old times, recall the good times. Don't talk about your divorce. There will be plenty of time for that later.

- If you discuss anything with your children (depending on their age(s)) reassure them that you love them and that you will be with them. They cannot afford to have the parents introducing emotional as well as physical stress into their lives.

- If you are innocent of something that you were accused of, do not let it go by the wayside, regardless of how trivial you think it might be. Gather you facts, organize your thoughts and communicate these things to your lawyer. Being able to show that your spouse is lying, fabricating stories, or making false accusations, is one of the most important activities that will need your undivided attention. You may not realize it at the time, but the little things can pile up against you and in time could even influence a judge, jury or mediator. As it did in my case.

Chapter-IX: You're Not Alone

We have all had tough times throughout our lives where things did not go as planned. It seems the only luck we have is bad luck. Hopefully, you are in a position where your family or friends help you through those rough patches and consider yourself extremely fortunate. For many of you, including myself, you have lost your support network. Family, friends, and associates would rather stay out of all the gory details. This can leave you with feelings of loneliness and abandonment.

Even though this could very well be the darkest time for you in your life, you need to reach back and stand tall. Remember, if you give up if you lie down without a fight, then they win. That would justify all their lies, all their accusations. That would be like pleading guilty to a crime which you never committed. You have the conviction to overcome, say it "I will not run!"

If you are going to take one thing away from this book, remember this, never give up, keep pushing forward. Fight for what is right, fight for your dignity. Most of all, fight to remain a part of your children's lives.

These are Tough Times

We have all experienced what we might consider tough times. Times where a particular situation brings us down, affects our family, or challenges us to find a solution to bring things back in balance. In most cases we persevere and work through to a solution which works for you and your family. I'm talking about life altering events, events which could take years to settle. One of them is what this book is all about, surviving the divorce and being able to move on with your life. Another being the challenge of living with a mental health issue, like ADHD.

Several factors can increase the complexity of a divorce, like how long you have been married, do you have children, what ages, what is your financial position, debt load, etc. Add onto that the degree of anger, hatred, and sheer contempt your spouse may have for you will be directly proportional to the level of stress, anxiety, and wear and tear on your physical & mental health which you will have to endure. There will be times where you will even start to doubt yourself. Don't be surprised if family and friends, and even your children may find themselves turning on you because of the perception which they have been told of you by your spouse and others within her support team. These can be the hardest times you may ever face. You must be mentally and physically prepared to survive for the long haul.

Take A Little Time for Yourself

A divorce is a grueling, draining, and exhaustive series of long emotional days. There are days when you see your life falling apart, you start doubting what the future will have in store. When this happens, it is time for an emotional time-out! For me it's great songs, and great movies. I found that for these short breaks, or interruptions in the madness give me comfort and hope for the future. It's these distractions from reality that refocused me and allowed me to keep moving forward. They have helped me through the day, reenergizing me to better handle the next day.

These are the movies that make me laugh and even make me cry at times. They remind me that hard work and determination can persevere against the odds. They help me visualize what it will take to keep me going and having the energy to turn things around if needed.

You may be thinking that this is an odd thing to see in a book about brutal divorces and dealing with mental health, but that is why this is mentioned. We all know life can be hard, but then add to that going through or just finishing a divorce, or having to deal with mental health issues, life can be that much more challenging. A lot of times we get too tunnel focused, to wrapped up in the everyday chaos. We forget that not only does our body need to reenergize, and so does our mind. We need something to distract us from all of the foolishness.

The entertainment industry provides us with such a distraction. So, grab a beer, nice glass of wine, cuddle up with the dog, or whatever relaxes you, and lose yourself for a few hours. You will feel better for it. Here are some great movies that can inspire you.

"Perseverance"		
10.	One Flew Over the Cuckoo's Nest	-
9.	Shawshank Redemption	-
8.	We are Marshall	True Story
7.	Moses	True Story
6.	Radio	True Story
5.	Miracle	True Story
4.	Awakenings	True Story
3.	The Rookie	True Story
2.	Rudy	True Story
1.	Unbroken	True Story

Then there are times where we get into that mood where we just want to see the good guys kicking some butt out of the people that got it coming to them. For me, these "get even," revenge type films fit the bill nicely. Not to say that there are dozens of other great flicks that would fall into this category. I'm sure you have some great ones that you might have on your list. Not that I'm suggesting or promoting violence, or any other physical actions against your spouse. These films are a nice distraction from everyday living.

"Butt Kicking Revenge Films"		
10.	Munich	Spielberg
9.	The Sting (1973)	Newman, Redford
8.	Gran Torino	Eastwood
7.	The Punisher (2004)	Jane, Travolta
6.	Law Abiding Citizen	Butler, Foxx
5.	Walking Tall	Johnson
4.	The Brave One	Foster
3.	Taken	Neeson
2.	John Wick	Reeves
1.	Kill Bill: Vol 1 & Vol2	Thurman

I also love a good Romantic Comedy, "chick flick" as some may call them. These are stories that will make you laugh and feel good. They even give us hope that one day, we too may find that person to have a relationship with. When the divorce theatrics end, and they will, you will be able to move forward and start to rebuild your life.

Romantic Comedies		
10.	What Women Want	Gibson & Hunt
9.	Crazy, Stupid, Love	Carell, Gosling, Moore, Stone, Tomei, Bacon
8.	Hitch	Smith, Mendes, James
7.	She's Out of My League	Baruchel, Eve, Miller
6.	Notting Hill	Grant, Roberts
5.	Moonstruck	Cher, Cage, Dukakis
4.	Groundhog Day	Murray, MacDowell
3.	Grease	Travolta, Newtown-John
2.	Married to the Mob	Pfeiffer, Modine
1.	Overboard	Hawn, Russell

No matter what your movie genre, taking that well needed break, will allow you to release those real-world stresses. It will help you clear your mind and recharge. You will be more alert and focused for the next day. Remember we can only take one day at a time. Do your best to tackle today and try your hardest to prepare for tomorrow. We can't have all the answers especially when we don't yet know what all of the questions are.

Be Open to the Possibilities

We never know what is in store for us. We never know who we may meet and where it will take us. There will be times where you will feel lonely, and these are normal feelings. Remember, you don't always have to be looking for something to find it!

No matter what the circumstances around the divorce, our lives will have changed. Change is not always easy to deal with. I do have to say though that when I look back, I have had a lot of changes in my lifetime, and many of them turned out to be good changes. Some doors had closed, but others will open and bring new experiences, new friendships, and new opportunities.

It is human nature to want to share our lives and experiences with someone who we care for and who cares about us in return. However, we also know that these things do take time, especially the older we get. I believe that they will happen if you remain positive and open to being able to recognize them when they do cross our path.

I look forward to the day that I will be able to share my life with someone. However, in my case, I also hope to be able to mend my relationships with my children. They were wrongly brought into the middle of a divorce between their parents, it was not their divorce. I think they should be allowed to judge for themselves what really happen, based on the real facts. Maybe they think they already have. It is something that I never thought I had to worry about, but it did happen, and it caught me completely by surprise. I pray that one day there can be some form of a dialect with my children. I cherish the memories which we shared, the memories they may have chosen to suppress. In the meantime, I will wake up every morning to a brand-new day, knowing that there are endless possibilities which await, I only need to remain open-minded, stick to my plan, and my goals can be achieved.

It's hard to be candid with other people about your divorce, It can bring on feelings of embarrassment, guilt, and self-doubt. Society has painted divorce with the persona of being associated with failure, and that of being a "loser," but in many cases this can be the farthest thing from the truth. In my case it still did not change the fact that I did not want to burden my friends and family with my problems. However, this only left me with increased feelings of loneliness and despair.

It is going to be hard at times. For me I dedicated the past thirty-two years of my life to my family, other than work, I did not have much else. Over the years, having to focus 100% of my free time on the needs of my family, causing me to lose touch with my friends, and many of my relatives. Most of all though, I lost touch with myself and who I really was and what I was all about.

Divorce is a second chance at life. It is an opportunity to gain back some of the things that you may have lost along the way during the time you were married. Maybe you gave up your love for working on muscle cars. After the divorce you will have that opportunity to gain part of yourself back. Pick up that project that you may have shelved years ago or start the one that you really wanted to but never did. Call that friend you lost touch with; you will be amazed at how good it will make you feel. For me it was about my low self-esteem. Over the years I gained weight and hated the way I looked. So much so that I could not stand looking in the mirror or having anyone taking a picture of me. When the divorce was finally all over that is the first thing I addressed. Heading to the gym every other day, and before I knew it the pounds were coming off. In the end I lost thirty seven pounds and it felt great. One night, around two am, I went on a buying spree, buying twenty one new shirts. I lost so much weight that I was able to get rid of all my extra-large shirts. It was well worth every penny that I spent.

Having free time to focus on myself for a change allowed me to dust off the golf clubs and start playing on a regular basis. I can think of no better place then Florida. I had pretty much given up the game, as it was expensive, and required too much of my time. Since moving to Florida, golf has opened opportunities to meet a lot of new people, make new friends, and forge new relationships. Who knows maybe, it will lead to something more.

The one thing about the divorce that tour me up inside was the fact that my children bought into all the lies and ridiculous stories that were told to them by their mother. It tormented me that my side of the story never got to be told. I took my newfound time to set the record straight. To take two plus years of notes and put them all together. This time no one was going to cut me off or not let me talk. This time I will have the final say. It's my time to tell it like it really happened. It's my chance to put it all out there for the world to see in hopes that my children will one day read this book and have their own awakening.

Importance of a Good Support Team

There is evidence that problems with peer relationships, peer rejection, bullying, and loneliness are risk factors for the development of affective conditions such as depression in adolescence. [7-4], [7-10] Conversely, high quality peer relationships appear to protect against mental health problems and strengthen adolescent resilience. Lessoning anxiety that may have even surfaced before the age of twenty-four. [7-3]

The science community identifies that social interactions are proposed to be a basic human need, analogous to other fundamental needs such as food consumption or sleep. Feeling insufficiently connected to others is associated with profound and lasting negative consequences on physical and mental health, even leading to increased mortality. [7-2]

Even though in some social circle this situation is not taken as seriously as others, it has been proven that the effects of limited human interaction can have negative effects on physical and mental health [7-5], [7-6],[7-7],[7-8],[7-9] These effects include:

- Higher risk of depression & anxiety
- Poor sleep quality
- Impaired executive function
- Poor cardiovascular function
- High blood pressure
- Obesity
- Low self-esteem

This is a serious list. In my case I gained over thirty pounds, my blood pressure climbed to 190/110, I was told this was getting into very serious territory and could start affecting my overall health in multiple ways. I wasn't leaving the house much, I was distracted from my focus on work, which really bothered me as that is one thing that I am very proud of. In general I had a lack luster feeling about myself and the desire to get involved in things. I could feel what was happening, but I lacked the motivation and drive to turn myself around.

I was so distracted by having to investigate and prove all of the things that I was accused of that I really didn't pick up on the impact that all of these things were having on me. Even with the medications that I was taking the overwhelming feeling of loneliness and abandonment was hard to manage. As the days, weeks, and months passed by I saw my relationship with my children slipping away. Their mother was tightening her grip on them and driving home these fictious stories. I guess it was easy to blame me for everything that was happening to the family and all of the bad things that had happened to them.

The divorce was definitely taking its toll on me. I'm normally a very upbeat happy person, but being surrounded by all the negativity and isolation was beating me down, it was overwhelming to handle. I'm not one that turns to alcohol when I start feeling down and depressed, I never was, but I will tell you it was very tempting. I've always had an additive personality, but I was always able to turn my focus to work instead of the other more dangerous possibilities.

Going through a divorce is a lonely feeling. In many situations, you may be isolated away from the very loved one who you cared for, took care of, and supported for years, or in my case, decades. When you feel yourself getting down, you may look around you and find yourself alone. It is times like these where you must focus. Take this time to reach out to a friend, maybe there is someone who you haven't spoken with in a while. That doesn't matter, because true friends will understand and will be there for you, no matter what. Only when I look back at everything do I realize how lost I was at times.

The constant badgering, the endless lies and accusations, from my spouse and her legal team was exhausting. I had lost myself, my self-worth. Not until I broke free from that life did I begin to realize that I do have a lot to offer others. Being away from Connecticut allowed me to experience things that I had not in decades. I started to feel vibrant and alive again. I started to build motivation and purpose for my life. My senses were exploding with the excitement I was feeling. I turned my depression my children cutting me off, over to working out at the gym. I finally had the extra funds to Address problems with my teeth that I had been putting off for the several years. It had been over twenty years since I felt good about myself. I was proud of the strides that I have made, and it felt great.

Making Lasting Friends

It's naturally harder for men to make relationships with people compared to women. It is going to help you a lot if there are "outsiders" which can support you, and your claims. During the course of the divorce things are going to be said, and accusations are going to be flying around. Having another person who care "bear witness" in your favor to things you have said can be very impactful, especially if your case ends up in a court trial.

Everyone makes new friends throughout their lives. However, few of them are lasting relationships over the long haul. For most of my adult life it has been easy to meet new people and have a comfortable conversation. We may have the opportunity to see these same people on a regular basis but it's usually around the event, which hooked us up in the first place. Like the kids soccer team, or marching band team. Now when you look back at all of these, how many really became long-term? A lot less than a women experiences when they meet new people.

As parents one of these stages is during the time our kids are growing up. Usually around the clubs, sports, or affiliations in which your kids are involved in. For the working parent it can be a challenge, they don't have as much "free" time, having to spend most of their time working. If you and your spouse both have a day job, it's even tougher to form new relationships, especially the more meaningful kind. We see other parents at our children's events, we have cordial chit-chat and then the event is over, and we whisk off to the next event. From a man's perspective it is harder for us to be open to new people as our time is primarily focused on work and surviving the next day.

Now don't get me wrong, I have met great people through the years my children were growing up, but from a guy's perspective, they just don't advance into that zone where you can really talk about more personal things then what specifically the kids are involved in, or "how's work going" type conversations. Some relationships last longer than others, but for me most of them slipped away over time.

You then end up with having a limited number of people which you might go to during tough times. Like when you are going through a divorce, or even when you may find out that you are struggle with the challenges which life throws at us from time to time. Women on the other hand, especially those that have been lucky enough to not have to work, they are around your children for most of the day, every day. They are able to build deeper relationships with the other mothers. Relationships that often last well beyond the school year.

You will find that relationships between men & women are different. Why Does it Matter? Studies have shown that who we become friends with falls very much in line with basic common sense. We are more likely to become friends with people who are trustworthy, have similar likes and dislikes, and who live physically close to us. Now the internet has made a big dent into needing the physicality aspect as vital to having a good friendship. People also prefer friends who are fun to hang out with. We prefer to be friends with people who makes us feel good when we hear from them or get together.

It has been noted in numerous studies, having friends freely generates more feelings of happiness, even more so than family, religion, or success in one's career. However, the 'depth" of these relationships very much does differ between how men and women define and manage these relationships [7-1].

Many experts agree that men, unlike women, tend to prefer more activity-based friendships while women tend to prefer more friendship types. Although the dynamics of male-male friendships and female-female friendships are more similar than they are different, there remains a difference in how the gender's view and engages in friendships. While one is more casual (male friendships), the other is more intimate and personal (female friendships).

Not surprisingly, female friendships tend to be more dependent on face-to-face contact, are more emotional, include the sharing of thoughts and feelings, and include more support. Friendships between males tend to be more side-to-side rather than face-to-face. Males tend to value relationships that include shared activities, are less intimate, and transactional. [7-2].

Unlike women, men often do not feel the need to discuss all the changes in their lives with a friend or a need to stay in touch. Interestingly, men can go extended periods of time, months or even years, without having contact with a friend, yet still consider the other person a close friend. In contrast, if a woman does not have regular contact with an individual she views as a close friend, then she is more likely to assume they have grown apart, is no longer interested in the friendship, and assume the friendship is over.

Although, male friendships tend to lack intimacy, they are less fragile than female friendships. Men are more likely to bond by engaging in shared activities, such as sports (side-to-side), while women tend to bond through the disclosing of secrets, talking, and spending time together (face-to-face). It should be noted, men tend to make friends easier as they do not question the motives of the other person or feel the same pressure to disclose personal information to maintain the friendship as do women. While men may not share their inner-most feelings with their close male friends, studies have shown they are more apt to share these feelings with a wife, girlfriend, sister, or other platonic female friends.

These are important delineations during the period of a divorce, and thereafter. We are not equipped to properly deal with things like you losing custody or visitation rights with your children, or other extreme emotional occurrences. Having your children turn against you to the point where they want nothing to do with you is something I would never wish on anyone, nor want any child to have to live through. Being able for a man to share his feelings about the impact of such event fall outside the boundaries of a normal male-male friendship. Not having the same strong support group as your female counterpart just increases the stress and anxiety throughout the divorce proceedings.

Remember though, storms come and go, but the sun does rise the next morning. Each new day brings the spirit of hope to the situation, and the opportunity to change the status quo. Think about if today was your last day? Would you waste it?

There is no harm in reaching out to old friends or confiding in a coworker. You should not feel ashamed that you are in the middle of a divorce or just completed one. You will be surprised how people will react to you. When they see that you are confiding in them. People will surprise you, when they see that you need a friend, or shoulder to lean on, or just need not to be alone for a little while.

Being alone is not always a terrible thing. Life can get hectic, too fast, too overwhelming. It is OK to call a time out for yourself. It is OK to do something that allows you to unwind a little. However, also do not hesitate to pick up the phone and give a friend a call. I'm sure they would enjoy, catching a movie, have a beer or glass of wine, watching a ball game, or simply shooting the breeze with you. Take advantage of this time, turn a negative into a positive, live in that moment. Do not think about the divorce, do not think about work, use this time to relax and recharge.

Whatever you might not have been able to tackle today, can always be addressed tomorrow. Do not feel guilty about taking this time for yourself. You have worked hard taking care of your family for years, now it is time to take care of yourself.

Life is hard for all of use, some harder than others, but to succeed you have to fight through it.

"Lose Yourself"

His palms are sweaty, knees weak, arms are heavy
He's nervous, but on the surface, he looks calm and ready
To drop bombs, but he keeps on forgetting
What he wrote down, the whole crowd goes so loud
He opens his mouth, but the words won't come out
He's chokin' how? Everybody's jokin now
The clock's run out, time's up, over, blow
Snap back to reality, ope, there goes gravity
Ope, there Rabbit, he choked, he's so mad
But he won't give up that easy, no, he won't have it
He knows his whole back's to the ropes, it don't matter

No more games, I'm a change what you call rage
I was playin' in the beginning, the mood all changed
I've been chewed up and spit out and booed off stage
All the pain inside amplified by the
Fact that I can't get by with my nine-to-
Five and I can't provide the right type of life for my family
'Cause, man, these dame food stamps don't buy diapers
This is my life and these times are so hard,
And it's getting' even harder
Caught up between being a father and a prima donna,
I've got to formulate a plan or end up failed
Success is my only mother option, failure's not

You can do anything you set your mind to, man

8-Mile
Eminem

Conclusion / Lessons Learned

- Hopefully, you are picking up one of the common themes of how to survive your divorce and that is to be prepared for the unexpected and reach out to others that can help support you.

- Be open to new relationships.

- It's never too late to give an old friend, or girlfriend a call.

- In general, most women are more social than men when it comes to forming new friendships. If your spouse does not have to work then they will certainly have a larger support network to lean on, but do not let that get you down. Do not be hesitant to reach out to family and friends on your side to help you stay focused, calm, and determined.

- It is important for you to realize that you too have people that will support you and be there for you when things start getting rough. Friends that you can share anything with. They are supportive, not judgmental. No matter how long it may have been, real friends will be there for each other, no matter what. They will understand what you are going through. They can help get through the tough times ahead.

- Do not be afraid to confide in people, they may surprise you. It is unhealthy to keep everything pent up inside of us. You need to release those emotions. Once you can let go built up frustrations it will be easier to move forward beyond the divorce chaos.

- Do not hesitate to involve your lawyer, even when it comes to non-legal matters. This is the person that is going to become familiar with your entire life leading up to the filing of the divorce and will be in your corner until the end.

Chapter-X: I Get Knocked Down

Depending on your specific circumstances, your divorce proceedings will be different from anything you have experienced before. Even though every divorce has the same end goal, there are no two divorces that are the same. One large difference can be if you have children that are minors at the time of your divorce. This can bring a custody battle, and subsequent child support and visitation rights into the focus. This greatly adds to the complexity of one divorce over another. Then there is the battle that your spouse could wage war on you. The division of assets and liabilities is one major area that will get addressed. We never really know how it's all going to play out until we are smack dab in the middle of it all. There will be times where you get blind-sided, it's going to knock the wind out of you. Be ready for it, and remain calm, form a game plan with your lawyer to address the matter. Don't let it distract you. Many times that is their intension, is to distract you, throw you off your game.

You might be in a situation like my own, where I was severely penalized by the court system for providing a situation where my spouse did not have to work throughout most of our marriage, in lieu of raising the kids. I know this sounds counter intuitive, but these are the facts. The Judge will consider your spouse's age, the ability to earn a wage after the marriage is dissolved, and the need for your spouse to be able to support themselves. Then they will assess what they think is a fair division of assets and determine the amount of alimony, along with the terms of the agreement. Any one or even all of these factors can have a larger negative impact on a settlement decree, especially if you were the sole source of income for your family.

If you haven't realized by now, I will say it again. History is well documented that our US court system is prejudiced against the husband, especially when children come into the equation. Even if you a respectable husband and good father, you are going into this divorce with two strikes against you. That is just how our system currently works. Maybe, this will change one day but today is not one of those days. You will need to make sure that you have excellent representation from your lawyer. If you have been less of a husband and a weak father, then you can expect a worse outcome. Same holds true if you were less than an ideal mother and wife.

There is no doubt that you are going to get bombarded with repeated accusations and lies, many that will shock you and take you by surprise. It is your ability to take that hit and come back stronger than before that matters the most. You must remember you are not alone. Take a breath, stand up, regroup, and fight back. If you don't, if you are too tired or worse to nice to fight back, I can guarantee you things will only get worse.

Be well prepared for this, do not be surprised, but remember you will get through this! Each time we get knocked down we grow stronger because of it!

"I Get Knocked Down"

Truth, is I thought it mattered
I thought that music mattered
But does it, bollocks!
Not compared to how people matter

We'll be singing
When we're winning
We'll be singing

I get knocked down
But I get up again
You're never gonna keep me down
I get knocked down
But I get up again
You're never gonna keep me down

I get knocked down
But I get up again
You're never gonna keep me down

Pissing the night away
Pissing the night away

He drinks a whiskey drink
He drinks a vodka drink
He drinks a lager drink
He drinks a cider drink
He sings the songs that remind him of the good times
He sings the songs that remind him of the better times

Oh Danny Boy
Danny Boy

I get knocked down
But I get up again
You're never gonna keep me down
I get knocked down
But I get up again
You're never gonna keep me down
Chumbawamba

It's Not as Easy as it Seems

You may be thinking that, why not go straight to the Judicial Court and end the divorce cleanly and quickly. This could be the cast for a select few of you out there. I have a friend who I met recently that was one of the lucky ones. He has kids, and his spouse had her own issues and let's say wasn't the best of mothers. She ignore all of the court documents and never showed for the original court hearing. In his case, he asked the judge, how many more appearance can she simply ignore before something is done about it? The judge agreed and ruled for the husband right then and there. Saving the suffering through any length of a trial or mediation. However, this is a rarity.

For most of us it's not that simple, not that straight forward, and certainly not as painless. One of the reasons clearly involves the relationship that you and your spouse have during the time towards the end of your marriage. Add on top of this the possibility that your spouse wants to draw these proceedings out in order to gain a more favorable outcome for themselves. Be prepared and try to address each matter as soon as it arises, so that you can eliminate as much "in-between" time as possible. The time where one party is waiting for the other side to respond to a request. Remember it's not as simple as you answering an e-mail back. One thing you should never do by the way. Everything should be going through your lawyer. This just adds a layer of waiting for issues to be resolved.

Remember the length of time that it takes for your case to get settle is directly proportionate to the complexity of your case and the willingness of both sides to want to come to an agreement. Your spouse is going to try everything in their power to get the most out of you, come settlement time. This includes lying, embellishing stories, fabricating the facts, any means of distraction possible. They will take every opportunity to paint you as the evil, deadbeat parent, and a mean and thoughtless spouse. Don't be naïve that your spouse would never do such a thing! It's amazing what people turn into when they are confronted with change. In my case, I would have never thought my spouse would be as selfish and greedy as she turned out to be. Never would I have thought that she would involve our children in any of the gory details of our case.

In a large majority of the cases, having legal representation is critical in getting a fair resolution. The longer you have been married, the more complex the circumstances can be. Going into a jury trial situation can be costly, sometimes, into the five-figure range, depending on the particulars of your situation. Mediation is an alternative to a jury trial, that could save you thousands of dollars and end up yielding a resolution in much less time. the that being Mediation. Mediation is a legal settlement but without the complexities and cost of taking your case in front of a judge .More about mediation a bit later.

Our judicial system is not always fair. When there are children involved, under the age of eighteen, the deck is surely stacked against the father. Unless there are extreme circumstances where the mother is no longer present, or has issues with addiction of some kind, you are most likely going to lose out right custody of your children. You might want to start realizing this is a serious possibility. If you try to do whatever it takes to gain custody and the judge grants custody to your spouse anyway, you may lose more than you ever imagined. My suggestion, be the initiator of trying to work out an amicable settlement when it comes to the future of your children. You don't want to risk being shut out from your own children's lives.

Multiple studies have shown that a home with one of the parents not actively involved in the parenting duties, will negatively affect the children. You both need to remember this. The children's well-being is far more important than any amount of money or possessions which you may be fighting over. This is yet another reason that you nor your spouse should involve the children in the details and particulars of your divorce.

Is a Trial in Your Future

There are two different approaches that you can take that will decide the outcome of your settlement. The first is an expensive court trial, and the second being mediation. Going to court will cost you a lot more, compared to going the mediation route. During a trial, both parties get to tell their story in fine detail, that can take multiple days to conclude. Your spouse will try and paint the worst possible picture that they can in describing you and your marriage. Doing whatever it takes to get as much awarded to them as possible. Then you will have your time to rebut any claims that you felt were incorrectly stated by the other side. This back and forth will continue until the facts are heard or until the judge puts a stop to it, if he thinks the argument is not going to get resolved by itself. Either way that clock is ticking at some $300-$500 plus an hour, not including court costs.

If your spouse did not work for much of the marriage that works against you. The older they are the more likely the judge or mediator will be in determining that person's ability to reenter the work force. Hey, I get it, if I were not working for a long period of time, I would not want to have to go out and find a job. However, that would still not make me turn to stating false accusations and outright slandering as my spouse chose to do to get a more favorable resolution.

However, if your family includes having children, specifically minors, under the age of eighteen, having one or both of you trying to punish the other by involving the children, runs the risk of causing irrefutable damage to their own children. The children hear these false claims and accusations, and they take them for the truth, that can generate all sorts of hatred towards both their parents. It can also generate a general mistrust in the opposite sex when it comes time for them to have a relationship of their own.

You would think that the last thing a parent would want for their child is to damage their children's mental and/or physical state. However, vengeance and greed are ugly intentions that can get to the best of us. Only bad things can result from staging this kind or reply. At least this was the case with my divorce.

Going through with a trial, usually will be publicly humiliating and end up with both sides hating each other even more than before the trial started. This may be fine if you are never going to see each other again, but when children are involved, this is never a good idea. Another thing about a trial is they are usually open to spectators. Anyone who wants to attend your custody battle may be able to do so. If a trial resolution has been selected to settle your case it provides an opportunity for each side to state their case. Unfortunately, at the same time it gives each party the stage to reenact their version of what they want others to believe is the truth.

You need to think about how all of this may play out. In the end don't think for a minute that your spouse would not use one or even all these tactics to gain favor with the judge, friends, and / or family members, while in the process trying to destroy you financially and emotionally. Remember the end game, it's about getting out of a marriage which has been over for some time, in the simplest quickest way possible. Is it worth the risk of a costly trial, what are the benefits you hope to gain?

Each person's situation can move the needle in one direction or another, so I don't want you to think one approach is better than the other, they are just two different paths that you can take. In my case I couldn't afford the costs of a trial, and I thought a trial would be a bit overkill, and all I really wanted was to end the marriage, simply and quickly. If I would have known all of the games and manipulation that my spouse was going to play, I would have and should have gone directly down the trial path. I would have at least been able to be heard, publicly. I would have been able to dispute all the false claims and accusations with everyone in the same room. I would have been able to discredit these claims on the record. I would have been able to ensure that my children would have heard and understood the real facts around the marriage. As it ended up my children only got to hear one warped side of the truth. It would have been well worth the extra money that it would have cost. I would probably still have a relationship with my children if I would have endured a full blown trial. In my attempt to end the marriage quickly and with a minimal an impact as possible to the family, I caused my own demise with my children. My saw the opportunity to isolate me away from my children which then allowed her to spin her stories and turn them against me.

Mediation could be an Alternative

Mediation, in contrast, happens behind closed doors and only the couple and their lawyers are permitted to speak during what is usually a day-long affair. The mediator is usually a former judge that is approved by the court system to act on the courts behalf. Their decision is binding and final.

Divorce mediation is an alternative dispute resolution process that allows divorcing couples to try and negotiate a mutually acceptable agreement with the help of a neutral mediator. A mediator does not have the authority to make decisions. Instead, a mediator works in a neutral capacity and attempts to facilitate agreement on any disputed financial or co-parenting issues.

Going the mediation route does allow both parties to air their claims, but the problem is you do not hear those claims, you do not get to rebut claims made against you, there is no face-to-face interactions between the two parties. Only the lawyers get to communicate with each other and the mediator. If you agree to the mediator's "recommendations," then once signed, you cannot request a trial after the fact.

You, your spouse, and your lawyers enter the room where the mediator takes 15-20 minutes to discuss how the day will unfold. I particularly liked the part where the mediator tells you all that the settlement usually does not end the way each of you want, but that it will end in a fair settlement. So much for being a "fair" settlement part in my case. Since my ex got to tell her story first, and I was not allowed in the room while she told her lies. This put me at an extreme disadvantage as the mediator was no longer in the mood to hear my side of the story.

The mediator will take each of you and your lawyer(s) in a room without the other. They will ask you a series of questions. This is where you are supposed to be able to answer his questions and explain any accusations which may have been brought up against you. Then you come back together, where the judge discusses his views of what was said by each of you. Then he meets with the lawyers alone while you sit in a room alone awaiting the outcome. It's pretty straight forward, but in my case I think that worked against me.

The mediator will help both parties to understand the priorities and issues involved in the divorce, try, and clear up any misconceptions, and possibly offer ideas for reaching a resolution. It's important to understand that the mediator does NOT represent either party. Their primary goal is to facilitate getting a resolution agreed upon by both parties. They are not there to protect anyone's interests. That would be something that your lawyer is responsible for. In most states, legal counsel is required.

The Benefits of Mediation

- Mediation typically costs less than litigation or collaborative divorce, and the lawyers have a much more limited role.

- Mediation is less adversarial than litigation which reduces animosity and can help preserve a working relationship; maybe!

- Mediators are usually ex-judges, so they are all too familiar with the divorce process. They can assist both sides in acknowledging feelings but not allowing feelings to control the decision-making process, or at least that should be the intent.

- You and your spouse have significantly more control over the process and the outcome than when the court is involved. This should create a more durable agreement.

- You have more input so that you can feel better about arriving at a final agreement that fair rather than having a rigid set of rules that guide your fate.

- Mediation is much less emotionally harmful and better overall on children if you have any. Children hate to see conflict between their parents and by showing you are working together; you can set an example and minimize any repercussions. This point is dependent on your spouse. They can still drag the settlement process out, making it difficult to come to a final agreement.

- You still have the option of going to court. Choosing mediation does not in any way cause you to lose your right to litigate your divorce in front of a judge. Anything that took place during mediation will remain confidential (except for signed written agreements and financial declarations of facts). If at the end of the mediation process the two sides cannot come to an agreement, then you can still proceed to a full court trial.

- Mediation may still be an option even when domestic violence is present in the marriage. Whether mediation is appropriate really depends on the extent of the domestic violence and the imbalance of power. It is recommended that your attorney's be present as they will be able to provide clear guidance to the mediator in a manner which should facilitate the solution.

- A mediator can't order you to do anything. All that is required to make a divorce mediation successful is for both parties show up willing to negotiate and be open to compromising.

- The primary benefit of divorce mediation for fathers is that they are more likely to end up with greater access to their children, in most cases.

How to Prepare for Mediation

Mediation is voluntary, so both parties must agree to go this route. Once agreed upon, the key to a successful mediation is preparation. At this point you may have already provided your attorney with most of the hard financial facts, but you still need to have the reasons that surround the facts. Things that support the overall conditions that existed during the time you were married.

The Mediator is a person just like you and me, a person that is going to hear both sides and try to stay impartial. However they are still outsiders and new to all of the details of your case and your marriage and since the mediation only lasts a day, there will only be time to hit the high points. The problem with this is that this can then boil down to who gets the mediators attention and who grabs their attention. They are still suspectable to emotions and experiences which they have already had in their lives. This is the wild card in all of this. That is not to say that litigation would be any different and the judge may also be sensitive to certain prejudices.

Emotions and manipulations will surely take place as the parties try and discredit the other. If you're concerned that your spouse is less than forthcoming with accurate information, it will be up to you to make sure you get the attention of the mediator. It's a funny thing about the truth, it's black and white. Things happened or they didn't! Making sure the facts get heard should be paramount as they should dictate the outcome of your settlement. However, we live in the real world, and there are times where things don't go the way that they are drawn up to.

In my case my spouse lied on her financial declaration of facts, not identifying a secret credit card which she had for over a year. No one knows what kind of activity was put on that card over the years. Add to the secret credit card multiple retirement accounts which I never knew she had until well after the disclosure stage was completed. How does someone fund four different retirement accounts, when they only had a job for approximately only 1/6th of the time we were married. One could surmise that she was funneling sums of cash away from the family and into her own private IRA accounts.

In my case my spouse had previously been married. A fact that she hid from our children for almost the entire time of our marriage. I saw nothing good coming out of the children knowing about it, so I never brought the subject up, never talked about it. Her first marriage lasted just over a year. Maybe she had insecurities from her first marriage, and that was the reason for her secret accounts, but still, that is not the foundation for what a healthy marriage is built upon.

The financial affidavit is supposed to be a sworn testimony of each parties' financial assets and liabilities. A legal document, where, lying under oath is considered perjury. For whatever reason, everyone including the mediator, ignored these omissions, and legal misguiding's when it came to my spouse sworn statements. The misdirection that she hoped to achieve she did. Her true character deflected and attention directed at me.

As previously mentioned, if you are the father the court system is heavily slanted in the favor of the spouse. If you are the sole financial provider, the longer you are married and the older that you get, the more slated against you the settlement becomes. If you were to ask me, I would say that they got this all backwards. Do not get me wrong, I'm all in favor of a fair division of assets and alimony settlement. But if one spouse has been providing virtually everything financially for his or her family, why should they be the one that also has to take the majority share of the financial burden? Especially when that same spouse was more than capable of getting a job that could provide needed support to the families financial situation.

With mediation your lawyer will have less time with the mediator than if it were a full trial. It's critical that you tell your lawyer everything about your marriage. The last thing you want is for your lawyer to hear about something behind closed doors. Remember you will not be in the same room as the lawyers as they are arguing each side of the case. Your legal council must not be surprised with anything that you may have done. Having something come up for the first time during the mediation process is only going to hurt your case and impact the final divorce settlement decree.

To be perfectly honest, looking back in the manner of how my mediation went down, I would have chosen a jury trial. In the beginning, it seemed like things were going to work out fairly innocently, but with every passing day things got progressively worse. I have lost track of how many out right fraudulent statements I was accused of that I later proved were false. However, no trial, no judge ever got to hear them. My spouse and her council only had to create doubt in the mediator's eyes. Remember in most divorces fathers are considered guilty only until they prove themselves innocent, and even then, it may not have mattered to the mediator or judge.

Don't be Afraid to Pivot

When the divorce papers were filed and I heard about mediation being an option over going through a full expensive trial, it seemed like a fair option. The intent of mediation is to bring closure to the marriage, quickly and more inexpensively than a full court trial.

In my case, being responsible for the entire financial burden of my family left me with zero free cash that a trial would require. This was my divorce, and I could not put the financial burden on any of my friends or family. Something that didn't get in the way for my spouse. Unbeknownst to me, she went to our daughter for a $10,000 dollar loan. Our daughter was only starting her career as a theater set designer. Of all her friends and family why would she throw our daughter right into the middle of our divorce? She had a well-off brother and sister-in-law that had very high incomes. While her parents were also well off and living a comfortable life. Why not borrow the money from them? Our daughter had her own challenges in building her own life. Why involve her in all of this, if it was not to gain her sympathy?

I guess this was my spouses plan from the beginning. Play the poor, helpless, mother who was wronged by their father. What kind of greedy, selfish person manipulates their own daughter against her father. It did take the two of us to have our three beautiful children. I guess she forgot that. I guess my spouse never stopped to think about how she would feel if her own children turned against her. Maybe once they get to read about the whole story they may have second thoughts about how helpless their mother really was and how they decided to treat their father.

To be perfectly honest, looking back in the manner of how my mediation went down, I should have chosen a jury trial. In the beginning, it seemed like things were going to work out innocently enough, but with every passing day things got progressively worse. I have lost track how many out right fraudulent statements that were made against me. Because I chose mediation there was no trial, no jury which got to hear my side of the story. My spouse and her council only had to create doubt in the mediators' eyes.

Remember, at *any* stage in the process, even during the final mediation, you can put a halt to the mediation and declare that the process is just not working for you and that you do not see a settlement coming out of it that will be something that you could live with. It's your right to go to a trial, until the time that you sign any such agreement, and don't let anyone tell you any differently.

I still thought it would all work out for the best, when in fact, I got the worst possible outcome. I desperately wanted the marriage to be finally over after eighteen long months, and I looked forward to putting this nightmare behind me. I could not stomach even one more day of this nonsense. I needed it over. If I would have known how this was all going to play out, I would have taken a stand and forced a trial. That was going to be the only way that the truth was going to come out for all to hear. It's a decision that I will regret for a long time.

Don't Forget the End Game

In the beginning of the divorce your lawyer framed out how the divorce process worked. Identifying the most important goal in the divorce is getting you legally divorced. You need to be able to move on with your life without the headaches of having your spouse hanging around your neck, dragging you further into darkness. This should still be your top priority, followed closely by the details of your settlement.

If children are involved how is the settlement going to affect them and your relationship with them. Keeping your family functionally connected is paramount to your children's mental health. The mediator will help shape the settlement with the proper lines of communication in place and help parents establish boundaries regarding their children. However, this only applies to children under the legal limits of 18-years of age. Anything over that makes your children of legal age, above the approach of the courts to dictate any policies.

Experts agree that one of the most crucial factors in your children's adjustment to your divorce is the relationship their father has with their mother. Ex-spouses who can resolve their differences amicably and who continue to interact cooperatively help protect their children from the negative consequences of divorce. Under such conditions, divorce need not be a traumatic event for children.

Unless of course, your spouse is particularly upset with the change in their lifestyle that is going to take place. One could argue that your spouse would do or say anything to limit the possibility of having to go back to work to support themself. Which is exactly what happened in my case. My ex was able to sell her lawyer and the mediator her story based on extremely limited facts and was awarded a settlement which swung over 80% of our assets in her favor. More on my settlement later. Even though she has turned my children against me (hopefully, only a temporary situation) I will eagerly await any opportunity to start that relationship up again.

Another word of advice is to get a handle on the finances that will remain, post-divorce. Start to create a budget, what you think you will be left with after the divorce is finalized. If you were the sole provider in the marriage, then you will most likely retain your employment position and your income after the divorce decree, less alimony, and less child support, if applicable. This alone can be a huge financial burden that you must plan for, if you are going to be able to move forward with your life.

Remember to create a plan which includes paying off any liabilities that were transferred to you as part of your settlement decree. Plan for a portion of each check going to paying down your debts before you start allocating those funds into the mainstream of your spending. Credit card interest can cost you hundreds of dollars a month alone. Get them paid off as soon as possible.

Build an accurate budget which reflects all your obligations. You may have been delaying these things. I know having the realization of all that debt is like a slap in the face every time you think of it. However, you need to look at it this way, every day you pay down those obligations you are inching closer to your financial freedom. Once out of debt your check will go further, and you can get back to a more stable financial position. You will have no idea how amazing it will feel to be liberated from all the financial debts that haunted you in the past.. Trust me when I say, you will be able to build your new life, and hopefully, you will be able to find someone special to share your life with.

Mediation is supposed to also help the couple communicate in a clear and normal tone. Learning how to listen respectfully, focusing on the relevant issues, and making a clear resolution path are important communication skills to possess in managing any relationship, let alone a hypersensitive situation like a divorce. In the absence of this third party, the couple often slips into the blame game. When children are involved it is more important that the parents maintain their amicable relationship and "win" as a couple rather than that one parent "winning" the disagreement. Mediation maintains the focus on getting to a fair and amicable agreement that both parties can agree on. It's important that both sides can minimize the resentment they may have for the other for the good of the children's mental health.

Finally, remember that the end game is also about getting a settlement in place which is best for the custody of the children, if minor children are involved. The mediator is supposed to protect the future relationship of the parties as parents. Spouses who end their marriage still need to continue to cooperate in parenting their children for years to come. Spouses who have mediated their differences and who remain friends have protected their relationship so that they can talk amicably the next time there is an issue related to the children. Spouses who have destroyed their relationship by becoming legal adversaries must resort to talking to each other through lawyers. Mediation is supposed to create a situation that will allow you and your spouse to end the marriage, leaving the family whole.

When Mediation Goes Sideways

In my divorce case, we chose mediation. At that time it looked like it was our only way to end the marriage. It did put an end to getting a settlement on the table. A settlement which should have been reasonably fair for both parties, but in my case, it didn't quite end that way. The mediator believed her elaborate stories, looked at her age, and deduced that she would not be able to reenter the workforce. They reflected this by giving her virtual all of our assets, virtually everything that I worked for across my entire career.

The lawyers, the court, our relatives, may have all been fooled by my ex's theatrics and believed that she was incapable of getting back into the workforce, but they seemed to turn a blind eye on the fact that she had a stellar education with a full scholarship from New York University. NYU only happens to be the ranked twenty-fifth of the top universities in our entire nation. NYU does not hand out a full scholarships lightly.

Yet, the mediator stated that she "no longer possessed the tools to be able to find a job in today's market." The mediator was not an expert in the field of computer software development. A field that is desperate for talented people with any Project Manager skills and a rich history of experience. Both of which my spouse possesses. Another thing in her favor is that more than ever before organizations are turning to senior resources with the pedigree and experience, with a major focus on diversity hiring. Even over the age of sixty, with a little refresher course around the latest technology, she could easily obtain a six-figure job with minimal effort within a short period of time.

If she does decide to go back into the workforce and is fortunate enough to pull down a lofty salary, it will not change the fact that she will banking a sizable monthly alimony check. I really hope that she does take this opportunity to get back into the workforce, because there is a moratorium on those alimony payments. As of my birthday, August 14th, 2029, I will be able to celebrate that the last alimony payment has been paid. Boys and girls can you spell "P-A-R-T-Y" ? Happy 67th birthday to me!

Finding that job hinges one major personality trait, and that is the applicant's passion and desire to actually want to get back into the workforce. Be it starting up again after a long break from raising their children or even for someone looking for their first job. It is no surprise that getting back into the workforce can be a challenge, but without the desire to want to do so, you will more than likely struggle with finding the right job for yourself. In my situation, my ex made perfectly clear to me, many times over, that she had no intention of ever reentering the workforce, regardless of the fact that she possessed all the necessary skills to excel in the position. Even near the end, when money was extremely tight did she have no regard for our financial position. As far as she was concerned that was all my problem.

She possessed all the skills that major employers are searching for, hoping to find in any applicant that they interview. She started as an internship while at NYU with one of the largest US banks. Then after graduation she continued employment at the bank as a senior program analyst. While at the bank she was in charge of a portion of a large project that building a replacement software solution that was to replace an outdated system that handled all of the securities traded over the stock exchange. After moving on from the bank she moved into a consulting position for one of the "Big-4" accounting firms, where she was sent to Canada to facilitate, and lead yet another large project. She was being groomed for eventually becoming partner material. Somehow all of this pedigree was ignored when I tried to bring it up to the mediator. They chose to believe her cries of a poor homemaker and ignored wife instead. This was one of the major factors that determined the level of alimony that she was going to receive over the next six years. The sad joke of it all is that with her experience and knowledge, she could reenter the workforce anytime she wants to. She probably already has, and she's just laughing at how she put it over on the judge and stuck it to me at the same time.

For mediation to work requires that both parties want to work out an amicable settlement, an agreement of how things are going to be defined after the divorce, and how future any interactions will be managed. For some, the mediation is a hope to get through the divorce as quickly and inexpensively as possible. For others it's a way to get at least some involvement by the judicial system in hopes of getting a fair settlement.

You must be honest with yourself. If you think that your spouse is in a state where the last thing they want to do is to negotiate a fair settlement, then don't agree to the mediation as an option to get that settlement. Go with your gut feeling, discuss with close friends and family. In the end if a trial gives you a better chance at a fair settlement, just know that it's going to cost you more to achieve those results, but if you feel you have a good case and that you need your voice to be heard, then a full trial is the way you should go. No amount of money is worth damaging the relationship you have with your children. Don't let anyone try and take that away from you.

Conclusion / Lessons Learned

- If your spouse has not worked during a majority of your marriage, you must remember that the longer you have been married, coupled with their age, the harder it will be for your spouse to find a job, and the larger of an impact it could have on the settlement agreement.

- The more time your spouse was able to stay home without working the more in favor the courts will be to your spouse's situation.

- Games will be played by your spouse during the proceedings. They will try and distract you with misdirection, frustrate you with fabricated information, while trying to know you off your game any way that they can. Your ability to focus and battle back, pushing the other side, forcing them to provide absolute proof of their accusations will definitely impact the outcome of the case.

- Mediation is one viable way to get a faster less costly settlement than going to trial, however it doesn't fit everyone's circumstances.

- Going to court will allow you to get more of your story heard. Your lawyers will be able to cross examine your spouse and ask her if she has any physical evidence to support her claims, accusations, and downright attacks on your character. Depending on the severity of what is made up about could be considered slander, in which case your spouse could be held accountable for damages. Regardless, everything said during the trial will be documented and recorded in transcript form and logged with the court system for anyone to see.

- Going to trial could generate unexpected results which might have a negative impact on your children. Resulting in possible damage to the relationship they have with you at the time. Once these things are aired in court they can noty be undone.

- Be it mediation or trial, try to be the better person during the process. Please remember to limit the exposure of the details of the proceedings that your children will have. This even holds true for after the divorce is finalized. At that point burdening your children with the finer details will only make things worse. It may also have permanent damage to their mental and/or physical health. Hopefully, your spouse will have enough common sense to do the same. Unfortunately, this was not the case for me, as my ex continued with the lies and accusations well after the divorce settlement was released by the court.

- Lastly, it's going to be hard, it's going to be exhausting, just remember, never give up fighting for what you think is right. If it's the truth it can't be wrong.

Section III: Living in the Dark

Imagine what it feels like to be a prisoner in a cell with no bars. You can see freedom just a few feet away, but you are paralyzed and can never get any closer to being released. You can feel the walls closing in, the stress building with every passing day. No one else can see these walls, and most people look at you in bewilderment as to what you are even talking about. This prison is even worse than being held in a physical cell. This virtual prison is everywhere, affects everything you do, and unlike a physical sentence where you have a release date, there is no end. The loneliness is overwhelming.

There are tens of millions of people out there that are feeling trapped and might not even realize why, not knowing how they got there and worse, not knowing how to break free. The fact is, life is stressful, and for some, it pushes many into a state of loneliness, and depression. You do not need to have a mental disorder to feel similar anxiety and pressures. Though having a mental disorder only intensifies the feelings that you are having.

I can tell you firsthand, how hard it is to stay positive on any given day. The challenges that even a single day brings. There are so many distractions in life, some so small that they go unnoticed by most people. For people like me each of these insignificant events can derail my thought process. Your mind shifts direction and now you are no longer thinking about what you were doing only a few minutes prior. Like when you are looking around for your car keys because you are late for an appointment. While looking for your keys you pass by the sink full of dirty dishes, then you find yourself washing the dishes. You may be further derailed by a second distraction, and then a third. Who know how much real time has passed. But I highly doubt you are going to still make that appointment. Then this brings on new stress into your day.

This was just a simple example of how frustrating it can be to have to deal with a mental disorder. The scary thing is for the people that don't even realize that they do have a mental disorder, and there are things that can be done to help them through scenarios like the ones I just. Someone who doesn't understands why little things upset them when they do not seem to bother most other people, can't take corrective measures to "recenter" their mind.

For those people who still wander around not knowing why these things upset them, they tend to want to recoil, stay away from similar circumstances. They will often limit their interaction with others. You find yourself being more comfortable alone, having less friends than most. You see this happening and you don't understand why. You isolate yourself, in hopes that you can minimize the frustration and anxiety that comes over you. As I got older, I realized that disengaging was not the answer, I had to tackle the issues head-on.

However, this revelation that I had, only came after I was already fifty years of age. My life would have been so much less stressful if I would have been evaluated earlier in life. I would have been able to better manage the stresses that having your own family brings. After being frustrated for so many years I wanted to find someone who might be able to explain why I struggled with things that most other never have to worry about. I admitted to myself it was time to seek professional help. It was only at this point that I was diagnosed with having multiple mental health issues.

Chapter-XI: Coping with ADHD/ADD

Attention Deficit Hyperactivity Disorder and Attention Deficit Disorder and are neurodevelopmental disorders most often detected in adolescence, but quite often continue into adulthood. In the United States between 2.5% and 4.4% of the population suffer from ADD or ADHD. People with ADHD may have trouble paying attention, controlling impulsive behaviors (may act without thinking about what the result will be), or be overly active. Some adults that have ADHD have never been diagnosed. ADHD is not an illness, it's a category that defines the symptoms that people with ADHD have in common. Since these are neurodevelopmental disorder there is nothing that can be "fixed" to eliminate ADHD. There are exercises and medications that allow the mind to adjust to the environment and activities that are happening around it. This provides for a higher quality of life with a lot less stress and frustration that often accompanies this disorder.

As defined by the World Health Organization, neuro-developmental disorders (ND's) are impairments of the growth and development of the brain or central nervous system that affect behavior, cognition, emotion, learning ability, self-control, and memory. They cause difficulties in social, cognitive, and emotional functioning. The most prevalent ones include ADHD/ADD, Autism Spectrum Disorder (ASD) and Cerebral Palsy. [9-6]

Another important note to be made is that studies have shown that comorbidity of other conditions is highly likely in individuals with NDs, which in simple terms means if you have a single disorder, you most likely have multiple disorders. In my case, I was confirmed with having ADD and being bipolar.

Tendencies

To best understand what ADHD is and the effects of having it. Let's look at a brief list of the tendencies that a person might display if they did have ADHD. Some of these seem innocent enough but think of how it would feel if you had to struggle them in various situations, like working a job for instance, or being on a sports team in school.

- daydreaming a lot
- frequently forgetting or losing things a lot
- squirming or fidgeting
- talking too much
- making careless mistakes
- taking unnecessary risks
- having a hard time resisting temptation
- having trouble taking turns
- difficulty getting along with others

Lasting Impact

Sadly enough, when I look back into my childhood and most of my adult life, I had trouble coping with most of these tendencies. ADHD/ADD in adults can cause difficulty at work, at home, and difficulties with relationships. Symptoms may look different depending on your age. Symptoms can become more severe as the demands of adulthood increase.

Even though only a small percentage of Americans have been diagnosed. This still accounts for twelve million adults. These only include the adults which have been professionally diagnosed. Think about the millions more that are going through life, struggling with its effects, and not even knowing that there is hope for them. Having to deal with these effects, but not knowing that the feelings are not normal is like living in a prison that you can never leave, nor ever escape from. For many people it could be the single thing that is holding them back from coping in today's society. The stresses caused by ADHD/ADD can often be a large part of the reason that is causing an individual such struggles succeeding or excelling in their life.

Expanding your knowledge of mental disorders, in this case ADHD/ADD provides an opportunity to help someone that you may see struggling with some of the symptoms I have previously listed. Sometimes a person just needs a nudge in order to make the decision to seek a third parties opinion or helping is assessing if that person's issues, anxiety, stress, ability to focus, are a direct result of a mental disorder like ADHD/ADD. Getting the diagnosis from a professional is the first step to improving one's life. I waited until I was fifty years old, and I look back now and realize all of the struggles I could have avoided if I would have only been open to seeing a professional earlier than the age of fifty.

For me, I grew up in a household where taking any drug above an aspirin was, let me say, highly frowned upon, regardless of if it was a prescribed medication or not. I was told if something bothered me, that I should "Get over it!" or one of my favorites was to, "suck it up, and deal with it". Now yes, we all know life can be hard, cruel, and heartless, but for that percentage of the people that struggle everyday with ADHD/ADD. It felt like a virtual jail term more severe than any normal man has had to endure in a real jail. It's something that until recently, relatively speaking, was never taken seriously by most. It was easy to throw labels at us like, "he's difficult to work with," or "he has no patience." Easy words to say, it allowed the people putting these labels on us the convenience of not getting involved. For many of the millions of people who must live with ADHD/ADD, they get thrown into the corner like a dirty old stuffed animal.

After I was diagnosed with having multiple mental disorders, they knew the areas of my brain that were more than likely being affected. This allowed the doctors to focus on coming up with a solution, a medicine "cocktail," which would lessen the effects of my disorders. This cocktail is made up of several medications that focus on specific areas of the brain that provide for our mental health stability. After living for so long with no explanations, I attribute the doctor and the medical cocktail with turning my life around. It stabilized my emotions which then allowed me to focus on improving my life. Like my doctor said, when prescribing the medication to me, "Relax, these are not happy pills." Then she made clear that I would still have to work at managing my neurological disorders on a daily basis.

Research also shows the neurological disorders are often conditions that persist throughout an individual's entire lifetime. These symptoms can be challenging to relationships, productivity, social skills, and communications. They can create limitations for a person and impact their abilities to function within society. I know they were in my case. I know they made dealing with simple family issues and events a lot more challenging.

It's a bit more complicated when a child is diagnosed as they have a little more trouble being able to assess how medication might be affecting them. Making the process of locking down the optimal medication and dosages more time consuming. It can also be more stressful for the family as trying to adjust so life can be easier for them can bring upon more stress for the parent and siblings. Studies found that parents of children with NDs report feeling a greater amount of stress than those with children without a neurological disorder [9-7].

You Can Succeed

You may be thinking that not being able to focus, not being able to finish things, and the other resulting behavior that affects people with ADD/ADHD have stood in the way of those individuals being successful. Some of the world's influencers had ADD/ADHD, including Albert Einstein. He is one of the more famous people who suffered from the mental disorder, ADHD. Next time you start to get frustrated with having ADHD/ADD, take a minute to center yourself and think of a way you might address the issue a little differently that would reduce the stress and turn your ADHD/ADD disadvantage into an advantage instead. It may not happen in the beginning, but as you continue to try and train your mind to think a bit differently in times of stress, you will start to see that it will make a difference. To the point where it make turn things around for you, just like it did for people like Bill Gates and Walt Disney.

This "hyper focus" has allowed many individuals, despite the challenges of their ADHD, to become incredibly successful in their fields. Listed below are other phenomenally successful people, many that have changed the world as we know it. They to struggled and overcame the challenges of having ADHD/ADD. [9-6].

Bill Gates – Entrepreneur & Philanthropist

Bill Gates, born in 1955 is the founder of☐Microsoft, and has a net worth of many billions. He also chairs the Bill and Melinda Gates Foundation, the world's largest private charitable foundation that has so far donated $35.8 billion to charity.
He with This Morning in 2016 about his decision to drop out of Harvard University in order to pursue his dreams and create a start-up company that we now all know is Microsoft. He also discusses his constant activity and extremely busy schedule in an interview with Warren Buffet. Where he felt he was more comfortable being very busy then not busy at all.

Walt Disney – Icon of the Animation industry

Walt Disney was one of the greatest entrepreneurs of all time as his presence is still felt even over 50 years after his death. He founded the Walt Disney Corporation and pioneered the animation industry where he was animator, writer, voice actor, and film producer. He took what were crude drawings and turned them into a brand that is now instantly recognizable worldwide. With ADHD, he was able to build an empire in animated films and expanded into amusement parks, making products that people loved and wanted.

Michael Phelps - Swimmer

Michael Phelps, a former competitive swimmer, and the most decorated Olympian in history, was diagnosed with ADHD at age 9. School was challenging for Phelps, who told People magazine that he found it difficult to sit still and complete his work. He took medication but found that swimming was the best way to alleviate his symptoms. Today, Phelps is a public advocate for mental health therapy, saying that talking to someone changed his life.

Jim Carrey - Actor

Several of the characters actor Jim Carrey has portrayed are, quite frankly, frenetic. The roles are grown-up versions of the class clown of his school days when he struggled in school due to his ADHD. It wasn't until he reached adulthood and achieved worldwide fame that he understood that he was dealing with mental health issues.

Today, Carrey speaks candidly about both ADHD and his clinical depression. His artistic talents — both as an actor and a cartoonist —have helped him cope with lifelong symptoms.

More Professional Athletes with ADHD
Terry Bradshaw – football
Michael Jordan – basketball
Shaquille O'Neal – basketball
Pete Rose - baseball

More Actors with ADHD
Channing Tatum
Zooey Deschanel
Woody Harrelson
Will Smith
Johnny Depp

Other Notables with ADHD
Alexander Graham Bell – inventor
Thomas Edison – inventor
John F. Kennedy – President of the United States
John Lennon – singer, songwriter, peace activist
George Bernard Shaw – playwright
Jules Verne – science fiction writer

Circular Thinking

Early on in life I found I had a passion for working with computers. I loved the challenges that working with a programming language presented. It became something I loved to do. It did present its own unique set of challenges. It's like playing a video game for the first time. There is a lot of unknowns, and a lot of new things happening at the same time. Like in the video game you learn the tricks, the back doors, the cheats and you conquer the challenges. The same applied to my young career.

Even before the doctors diagnosed my ND's. I realized I had my challenges and needed to find a way to figure out how to increase my focus or I would continue to have problems at work. I was determined to push myself until I figured out a way to manage better what I later discovered was ADHD/ADD. It was really hard and frustrating in the beginning. However, I knew failing again, was not an option, and in the end I figured out enough to get me to the next level, and that is all I needed.

If you find yourself in a similar situation, don't let anyone tell you that you are not able to do something, and try not to get frustrated. In my opinion, people with ADHD/ADD are probably more equipped to handle the challenges of successfully handling multitasking than people that don't have AHDH/ADD. OCD & ADHD myself, and now having done studying on the subjects, I know that people like me fall into this category where our minds are "wired", as I like to call it, a bit differently than people that do not have OCD & ADHD.

I took the sections of my problem solving abilities that I was good at and built a methodology around that. I noticed that when I was successful, the projects had the same characteristics. They were projects that other people did not want or where others had already failed. The projects were involved and seemingly had a lot of tasks to conquer before victory could be declared, and finally there were usually unrealistic timeframes in which to complete the project. If you boil this down to one motivating factor it would be that if I could achieve all three and deliver the project where others could not in the defined timeframe then it would be an impressive accomplishment and would increasing my value in the company.

Even if the project did not line up with the above characteristics where had the best chances to succeed, I would change the parameters of the project. I would push the timeline up which put more pressure on myself, I would expand scope to deliver more than what was originally requested and I would shorten the tasks into more manageable tasks that I could complete quickly which would keep me motivated to move into the next task, and so on. The key to all of this, the key to managing my ND's was to always have my mind busy figuring things out.

To achieve this I had to break up the tasks, limiting any downtime during and between tasks. But how could I do this? Quite often task require information from other people for me to push forward with a task. Easy, I would start up another task, then push that task through until either it finished or until it hit a delay. If it hit a delay, I would check in on the first tasks and if I was still waiting for information then I would start a third task. I called this looping through of tasks, 'Circular Thinking". Having multiple tasks always open simultaneously and looping through them as one hit delays allowed the work to keep my mind always occupied. It also allowed me to keep motivated, as there would also be tasks that I would be completing, and the project(s) would always be moving closer to completion. I know it sounds crazy, but it worked for me, it kept my ADHD/ADD in check.

When I looked back I found that having to meet tight deadlines with the challenge of multiple tasks motivates me. It somehow allows my brain to process it's maximum potential without introducing interruptions or distractions away from the tasks at hand. I found this keeps my brain focused for longer periods of time, while easily handling multiple tasks. As my brain is busy rapidly switched from task to task, there is no wasted time having to think where I left off with each task. My brain intuitively knows where that thought stream left off. I was processing the tasks in a virtual parallel state.

I am not trying to say that this has been proven in any scientific studies or anything like that. I can only speak for what I have seen works for me for the first thirty years of my career. I continued this approach even after I started taking my meds. I look at it like my mind is in continuous motion and shifts task by task, but because I have given it multiple tasks to process it has a much lesser tendency to get derailed. When my mind get naturally distracted it shifts to another task, but because there is other tasks to process it does not wander off into a random area of my brain, off task, like it might have normally done. I have loaded my mind with different paths to follow that instead of getting derailed, my mind just automatically switches to a path that has already been set up to be processed.

If you ask the average person, this would be a strategy that would makes their head spin. They might say that the jumping from one task to another doesn't allow them to focus properly. They absolutely have a valid point. But those "average" people don't have ADHD/ADD.

To be straight, not everything is sunshine and roses, there are days that even with my meds there will be days where I have trouble getting started with my workday. The meds allow my brain to process more efficiently without getting distracted. It's not a cure, if I forget to take the meds one day, my mind will not be as focused, and it will be distracted more easily. Some mornings I struggle to get started in that case I need to 'jump-start" my mind. I go to my open-items list to remind me of the things that are still yet to be completed. This allows my mind to shift focus from a neutral state into drive, if you will. Once back in drive mode my mind remembers the paths, tasks / project, that were still left open from the prior day. Without this "jump-start" my mind might remain in neutral.

I knew the "deal with it" approach told to me when I was a kid was not going to cut it once I got out of school. As I was not diagnosis with ADHD/ADD until I was fifty years old, I invented my circular thinking approach to problem solving. Struggled to keep a job past eighteen months I started to see that the circular thinking approach flipped my disadvantages with having ADHA/ADD to an advantage.

After discovering this approach I was able to excel in a work environment that I might normally might have struggled in. I became more successful at my job, but maybe more important I was able to learn and retain what I learned at an increased pace. This eventually led to my creating my own consulting company.

Conclusion / Lessons Learned

- It's ok to have the feeling of being overwhelmed with life's troubles. Often what makes these feelings difficult to deal with when you are alone. Not having someone to help share your anxiety and loneliness with only makes those feelings more difficult to deal with.

- If you have questioned something in your life that has always not felt quite right, then it's up to you to do something about it. You have to be the initiator, once you start down this road you will quickly see that there will be many others that are there to support you. Make the first move, doing nothing and expecting things to magically change is not the answer.

- You need to be willing to be true to yourself in realizing the impact that you have on your family. Even though these things might be manifested by emotions that you feel you cannot control.

- You need to be able to admit and confide in others that you can't do this alone. You need to enlist the help of a family member, friend, coworker, or mental health professional.

Chapter-XII: Understanding Bipolar Disorder

We constantly see the commercials. The drug companies have spent tens of millions of dollars advertising their drugs that help curb the effects of being bipolar. It is that widespread. I like these ads because they just do not try to shove the drug at us and say, "trust us." The commercial at least describes the symptoms of what it is like to be bipolar. Maybe the most challenging thing about helping people that are bipolar is getting the patient themselves to realize that they are bipolar, and that the feelings they may be having, depression, lack of motivation to even do the littlest things may not be normal, and that there is something that might be able to help them. they are bipolar. It makes sense that we cannot fix the problem if we don't know what's broken.

The National Library of Medicine identifies that bipolar affective disorder is a multicomponent illness involving episodes of severe mood disturbance, neuro-psychological deficits, immunological and physiological changes, and disturbances in functioning [10-4]. It is one of the leading causes of disability worldwide [10-5] and is associated with high rates of premature mortality from both suicide and medical comorbidities.

Two percent of the world population suffers from some form of bipolar disorder. This doesn't sound like much, but we are talking about a staggering 160,000,000 people worldwide. The illness commonly starts in young adults. The clinical manifestations of bipolar disorder can be markedly varied between and within individuals across their lifespan. Bipolar disorders (BDs) are recurrent and sometimes chronic disorders of mood and encompass a spectrum between severe elevated and excitable mood states (mania) to the dysphoria, low energy, and despondency of depressive episodes. [10-1]

Bipolar disorder rarely manifests in isolation, with comorbidity rates indicating elevated lifetime risk of several co-occurring symptoms and comorbid disorders, particularly anxiety, attentional disorders, substance misuse disorders, and personality disorders. The causes of such comorbidity can be varied and complex: they could reflect a mixed presentation artifactually separated by current diagnostic criteria. They might also reflect independent illnesses; or they might represent the downstream effects of one disorder increasing the risk of developing another disorder. [10-7] Similarly, subthreshold, and syndromic symptoms of attention deficit/hyperactivity disorder are also observed across the lifespan of people with bipolar disorder, but particularly in early onset bipolar disorder [10-2], [10-8]

The Scary Truth

In the 1970s, the International Classification of Diseases and the Diagnostic and Statistical Manual of Mental Disorders reflected the prototypes of mania initially described by Kraepelin. To meet the primary requirement for a manic episode, an individual must experience elevated or excessively irritable mood for at least a week, accompanied by at least three other typical syndromic features of mania, such as increased activity, increased speed of thoughts, rapid speech, changes in esteem, decreased need for sleep, or excessive engagement in impulsive or pleasurable activities. This was the benchmark for the initial diagnosis for the existence of a mental disorder in children and adults.

Looking back now, the previous describes many of my days, as far back as I could remember. When I first sat down with my doctor, only some ten years ago, I was 50 years old, and she told me that it was clear that I was bipolar, I really didn't think much of it. That was mainly because I really didn't understand what being Bipolar was all about. Then as the psychologist told me about the testing and my results it scared me, but as we talked about the effects and how they related to me and what could be done, I started to feel a sense of calming that I can't really remember ever feeling.

For over fifty years I struggled trying to control the drastic mood swings that the imbalance in my brain was causing. It was a constant battle, trying to keep it together, trying to fit in. Now knowing that there might be alternative that could bring my bipolar to a less intrusive state was very encouraging; I was ecstatic.

Getting Professional Help

When I finally realized that they was a chance for a real answer to be found to my general question of "why I was so different" I sought out a profession. With my prejudices from growing up, I was still nervous about taking drugs being the answer for addressing my issues, but I was willing to at listen to the professionals. My doctor explained that there was no doubt that I was Bipolar and that it was also not unusual that someone with bipolar disorder would also have other mental disorders. In my case it was also struggling with having ADHD. The doctor told me that the first challenge was to find the right blend of medication which would settle my brain down, calm my anxiety, and reduce my paranoia/stress. Once that was achieved, then finding the best medication that would work in conjunction with the mood stabilizer to address my ADHD would be relatively easy for them.

I will never forget the day that I tried the doctors first recommendation. They tampered their statements that the results may not be what I'm expecting and not to be disappointed. This was the first attempt at solving a complex problem. That morning, I took the meds and very quickly I had an overwhelming calm come over me, followed by a clarity, that then allowed solutions to work challenges that I was having to come flooding in. I felt no stress in the least. It was liberating. I was able to think clearly for the first time in my life. It felt so empowering. I get a little emotional when I think back to that day. Now, ten plus years later, I will remember that day like it was yesterday. It changed the rest of my life.

There was one side effect that I do have to deal. Since this medical cocktail generates the ability to have my mind have tremendous focus it doesn't allow it to shut down for a "normal' amount of sleep time. My normal night's sleep is only about 4-5 hours, and quite frequently that is not an uninterrupted sleep. On occasions I'm able to get a normal eight to nine hours. That only usually happens if I really get worn down during that day, or I have a very successful day where I have closure on the things I was working on throughout the day. This way my mind has nothing to latch onto.

I mentioned that I got lucky with the medication that the doctors prescribed for me. Not everyone with bipolar disorder, or other BN's or MD's is as lucky as I was. To these folks I say, don't give up, continue to work with your doctor. Keep a cheerful outlook, believe me, when I say that when you do find that combination that fits your body chemistry, it will be a day you'll never forget. It can be frustrating knowing that others have found that combination that works and blends with their chemistry, but there is hope. The scientific community is finding new medication and new combinations that are providing positive results previously not found in patients. I waited fifty years before I found the medical combination. Of course I wish I would have found it sooner, but I look at it this way, it changed the rest of my life, for as long as I live, God willing.

Living with a Mental Disorder

There are endless examples of great people who had a mental disorder. They conquered their fear, turned their affliction into an advantage that others did not have. They found ways to be able to keep the effects of their disorders in balance, call it what you will, this does not change the fact that without these great people, the world would be a different place today [10-9] Maybe this will make you look at yourself or someone you know just a bit differently. You must want it badly enough and want to keep fighting until you find what will make the difference.

There are other people out in the world that may be struggling with similar conditions that manifest themselves in different mannerisms, but still making everyday life more challenging to cope. It might not even be obvious to you. Like myself, I lived with my condition for fifty plus years until I figured it out. In my eyes, I just thought I was wired differently than most and that I had to find a way to deal with it.

Once the problem can be defined, the search for a solution can begin. Until this happens you may never be to move forward with clarity in your life. You will finally be free to eliminate the things that may have been holding you back from obtaining your hopes and dreams all this time. Having a mental disorder doesn't have to limit your success, it doesn't have to define you. It didn't for these great individuals.

Abraham Lincoln

The revered sixteenth President of the United States suffered from severe and incapacitating depressions that occasionally led to thoughts of suicide, as documented in numerous biographies.

Winston Churchhill

"Had he been a stable and equable man, he could never have inspired the nation. In 1940, when all the odds were against Britain, a leader of sober judgment might well have concluded that we were finished," wrote Anthony Storr about Churchill's bipolar disorder in Churchill's Black Dog, Kafka's Mice, and Other Phenomena of the Human Mind.

Michelangelo

The mental illness of one of the world's greatest artistic geniuses is discussed in The Dynamics of Creation by Anthony Storr.

Vasloc Nijinsky

The dancer's battle with schizophrenia is documented in his autobiography, The Diary of Vaslov Nijinksy.

Leo Tolstoy

Author of War and Peace, Tolstoy revealed the extent of his own mental illness in the memoir Confession. His experiences are also discussed in The Dynamics of Creation by Anthony Storr and The Inner World of Mental Illness: A Series of First Person Accounts of What It Was Like by Bert Kaplan.

Ludwig van Beethoven
The brilliant composer experienced bipolar disorder, as documented in The Key to Genius: Manic Depression and the Creative Life by D. Jablow Hershman and Julian Lieb.

Isaac Newton
The scientist's mental illness is discussed in The Dynamics of Creation by Anthony Storr and The Key to Genius: Manic Depression and the Creative Life by D. Jablow Hershman and Julian Lieb.

Lionel Aldridge
A defensive end for Vince Lombardi's legendary Green Bay Packers of the 1960's, Aldridge played in two Super Bowls. In the 1970's, he suffered from schizophrenia and was homeless for two and a half years. Until his death in 1998, he gave inspirational talks on his battle against paranoid schizophrenia. His story is the story of numerous newspaper articles.

Vincent Van Gogh
The celebrated artist's bipolar disorder is discussed in The Key to Genius: Manic Depression and the Creative Life by D. Jablow Hershman and Julian Lieb and Dear Theo, The Autobiography of Van Gogh.

These are only a handful of the great minds, creators, and artists of our past, there are hundreds more. By now you show start to see that it's not about a label that might be put on someone that may make them success or fail. It's the person inside that label that determines their own greatness.

Conclusion / Lessons Learned

- Having Bipolar disorder is not a disease. It's a disorder or condition where the connections in the brain are not the same as most other people. These differences make it difficult to cope with many of the stresses of everyday life, but they don't define us. They can be managed.

- You should not feel ashamed or embarrassed that you have a mental disorder. Hundreds of millions of people in this world do. Understanding the impact of being Bipolar is the first step to getting it under control.

- You can't do this alone. Seek out a doctor that will be able to work with you in assessing the issues and concerns you are having. It's quite possible that a medical solution might be available that could provide the balance that your brain requires.

- Understand that there are many alternative medications that can help reduce or eliminate the effects that you could be having. This itself poses a challenge in finding the right mix of medications that proves the right mix that gives you a total solution.

- Have someone that can be by your side to help you through this journey. A strong support network will easy the anxiety during this exploratory journey.

- It may not be easy, it may not be quick, but when you do find that medication which works for you, there is no describing the freedom that you will feel. You will see the world in a different light, while others will see the real you, and I know they will be impressed with what they see.

Section IV: After the Divorce Decree

The day that your divorce is finalized and stamped by the court, you will feel like a huge weight has been lifted off your shoulders. However, this feeling might be short lived. There is often items that were mentioned in the decree that still need to be executed. It might be the selling of your primary residence, division of the furniture and other assets or finalizing child support living arrangements. Then there is the transferring of funds from bank accounts between the parties. All of which takes a certain amount of time, which unfortunately can't be rushed.

You need to stay focused, because until these items are wrapped up, you will still have to interact with your now ex-spouse. You still must deal with open issues and validation that items get executed correctly as decreed in the divorce filing. You may be the only person that can do such a validation. Not even your lawyers might know that level of detail. Believe me I know how hard this can be, even with the medication that I was taking I had real trouble sticking to the tasks being asked of me.

In my case, the court had a separate hearing about the division of our assets, which included our furniture, and less any funds which were already part of the divorce decree. It was declared that we would sell an expensive Chippendale dining room set then split the proceeds. Once I moved out of the house, months before it was sold, who knows what ever happened to that set. Half the proceeds would have gone a long way to help be put a dent in all of the debt the court decreed to me. This is exactly what my ex did not want to happen.

Until you have wrapped up all the items, you will still be distracted. Keep on point and move through the process focusing on resolving the issue at hand. Until you check off each of the items you will not be able to move on with your life.

Chapter-XIII: Interacting with Your Spouse

The divorce becomes final, you have a huge sense of relief. The stress, headaches, and sick feeling in your stomach will lesson, and hopefully in a short period of time, disappear entirely. Even though the divorce process may be over there still may be more to follow.

If you have minor children, you may have ended the marriage, but you are now entering a new phase of parenting your children. If your spouse has custody, you may have the children staying with you on a limited basis per month, or you may only have visitation rights. If you want to continue the relationship with your children or improve the relationship after the divorce proceedings, stress of moving into another house and other things that could impact your relationship with your children, you must build a new interaction with your ex.

During my research, I have found some common themes around setting up your own standards when it comes to post-divorce interaction with your spouse. Specific guidelines need to be defined, both of you have to be comfortable with these guidelines and be able to stick to them after the divorce has been finalized. Do not just sign off on this part of the divorce settlement, as it is this part that extends well beyond the end of the divorce proceedings, the courts final decree.

Try your best to show respect, even if your ex chooses not to.

- Align to any legal instructions.

- Focus on the priorities What is best for your children's well-being should always come first, and then your particular needs would come second.

- Set ground rules that determine the nature of this new relationship you will have with your ex.

- Communicate with your ex via writing/texting and/or brief calls.

- Keep all communications limited to only what is necessary for the kids or legal matters. Try and avoid rehashing anything from the past.

- Speak to one another in respectful ways, especially around the kids.

- Most important, REMAIN CALM, especially if the children are around.

Above Reproach

I need to go back to the circumstances that surrounded our expensive dining room set. It was a perfect example that illustrated multiple areas where my ex disregarded the court's decree entirely, and the court then not wanting to deal with it after the fact. It's yet another example that as someone that might be going through a divorce or knowing someone that will be, you need to be wary of.

The way this supposed to work, as it was decreed by the mediator and signed by both parties as part of the settlement, was that we agreed on how to sell the furniture, and then split the proceeds. It was a fourteen-foot long Chippendale dining room set with ten chairs. The chairs along were $950.00 each to replace, not to mention a two leaf, three base leg dining room table, was appraised over $35,000! She never even mentioned the table. It mysteriously just disappear from the house days before the closing. Of course I was no longer living in the house, so I never was in a position to witness what happened to it.

One of two things happened, both of which violated the court agreement that we signed. Either she sold the set on the side, unbeknownst to me, and pocketed all of the money. The alternative action was that she "acquired" the set for herself. She always loved that set. So I would not be surprised if she sold it for some nothing cost of a hundred dollars or told me she donated it to some charity, so that there would be no proceeds, then have it moved right into her dining room of her new place of residency, or give it to one of her brothers, or friends. Either way I did not see a dime, nor was I giving any thought or asked to participate in the sale of the dining room set. She also disregarded the court's decree entirely, as if it were never documented.

Based on the divorce decree I was now responsible for virtually all our combined debts and left with virtually zero assets. Half of the proceeds of this amazing set of furniture would have gone go a long way to help pay down some of the debts. Why should I think that at this late stage that she would even consider what would be a fair and amicable settlement.

Point #1: Whatever she did she never communicated it to me nor my lawyers.

Point #2: When the house was sold and everything moved out, where did this furniture set go? No one seems to want to admit.

Point #3: Rumors had it that she sold it on Facebook Marketplace for pennies on the dollar so that there would be no proceeds to be split. Probably to a relative and then moved back to my Ex's new house.

Point #4: When the furniture magically disappeared, or was sold; was it sold to say a family member from her side and then this furniture found its way back into her next house?

This was yet another example of how she ignored the rules and actions dictated by the court if they did not favor her own gains. While making sure that what she did do would cause me more financial and emotional stress. The courts never followed up, and never did anything about it when I complained about it. In fact, the court decreed that this was not their problem, that I should go back to the mediator for this, as it was part of his final divorce decree. My lawyer had told me after she tried to step in that she very rarely had seen a court that did not add something into the official decree that the mediator requested to have added. She mentioned something like this happens less than 1% of the time. Was it really an oversight? I will let you decide.

The Evil that Lies Beneath

Why am I not shocked. I'm not shocked that my ex was this calculating. Heck she was with everything else in her plan. I'm not shocked that she wanted to keep the proceedings going as long as possible, so she could drag out the amount of time that she could stay in our house while I was left paying for all the bills. I'm not shocked that she came up with all of these stories about wanting the player piano we had, just to turn it around to sell it to some strangers. She did this because I specifically made this my number one item on the list of the division of our assets. A piano that my mother loved to hear play; and one that she was extremely excited to be able to add to her house in Florida. My ex had to find a way to stick it to my mother in this divorce. It wasn't enough that she turned the kids against their own father, but she turned them against their 85 year old grandmother and grandfather, who were innocent bystanders in this whole thing.

I walked into my mom's craft/sewing studio, to see hundreds of pictures scattered across the tables. She used to have this space as a sewing area, a creative place, one of her happiest of places to spend her time. But ever since her stroke and two heart attacks eighteen months ago, she can no longer function in that capacity. Instead, there isn't a day that goes by that I don't walk past this room to see her sitting in her wheelchair holding a picture or two, or three, of her grandchildren just quietly sobbing.

Sometimes she simple asks if there is anything she can do? What am I supposed to say to that? It makes me so angry. This woman, my mother, my children's grandmother would always come over our house to see my kids when we lived near each other in Long Island, New York. Then again when we moved ninety miles north to Connecticut. She loved the "pop-in" for a visit to see the kids. She would drive ninety miles by herself just too spend time with her grandchildren. She loves my kids with all her heart. She would make sure that her only granddaughter, Lindsay, would be sent a dozen roses for her birthday. Over and over, she tells me the story of when years back my daughter, surprised my parents by ringing their doorbell. Lindsay happened to be in Florida and thought it nice to surprise them. My mom was all smiles.

How can it be that my ex-spouse can sit there and rationalize how she is justified to play God; and steal away our children from their own grandparents. What evil, hurtful person would manipulate children so that their grandmother would be targeted so that she could never enjoy seeing her grandchildren ever again? It's unthinkable to me.

I can guarantee you that, to this day, my-ex makes sure she drives out with the kids to see her parents on a weekly basis. She really thinks that she is above reproach. One day my parents will no longer be around, and then it will be too late. I hope that one day before this my children will listen to their own heart and realize that this was wrong. They are good kids, adults now; not talking to me, sure. It eats away at my sole, but to treat your own innocent grandparents like this. That is not something that I would ever have thought would even be a consideration from my own children. This was their parent divorce, my parent had nothing to do with it and at no point even got involved in any of it over the eighteen months that the proceeds took to get finalized.

I pray every day that my parents will someday, get to be with and talk with their grandchildren again. I pray that my children will realize that no one deserves to be treated with the disrespect in the way that they have treated their own grandparents. I hope this moment comes before it's too late, at that time it may not to be able to be corrected. We have such a limited time on this earth, and to waste any of it is a waste of god's gift to us.

Maybe a miracle will happen. Just maybe, one day, my mom will open her front door and her grandchildren will be standing in front of her ready to give her a great big hug. Nothing needs to be said about the past. The past is behind us. We can only live in the present and look forward to the future. That would be a glorious day.

Dealing with Life's Events

Enough about my specific situation, what if your children are not legally adults yet? There will still be endless number of events that you will want to participate in, as the parent of your children.

However, the younger that your children are, the more complicated it can be in trying to get things to a state of "new normal." How will the children deal with parents living apart from one another. How will it work when children get sick or require things like parent teacher conferences at school. This is why it's crucial to establish those ground rules we talked about. Having these ground rules in place early on will eliminate a lot of bickering down the road. Other events that you should be planning is to how you two will deal with:

- Graduations & Weddings
- Birth of grandchildren
- Local and global emergencies
- Loss of employment/housing for either one of you
- Health issues of your children

You must find a way to communicate that works for both of you. In my case no direct communication was the best communication. Just about halfway into the divorce I cut off all direct contact with my there was no communications, as that would have just got in the way of my spouse's plan to ruin me. Now if your divorce unfolds like the way mine did, the likelihood of an amicable settlement for communicating will be slim to never. My ex did everything she could to drive a wall between our children and myself, their father. She made sure that she created enough noise that the judge/mediator had little time to listen to any rebuttals from my perspective when he decreed my complete pension be handed over to her and saddled me with a hundred thousand dollars in credit card debt. Debt that she mostly incurred by herself. Then the cherry on top of it all was granting her alimony equal to thirty percent of my future paychecks for the next six years.

Clearly you can see why this left little room for establishing any ground rules for communication between myself and my ex. To be honest, since our children were legally adults, there isn't much need to have any communication with her, and in my case this was a blessing.

However, I do hope and pray that one day my children will want to have some kind of relationship with me. Until then, my children will probably continue to shun my existence, not recognizing me as their father. I hope no one has to endure circumstances similar to these. You want to do another in your power to keep the relationships open with your children. Having your children turn on you, especially under false pretenses will rip your heart out, and nothing can ease the pain.

Managing Interactions with your Spouse

Here are four questions you may want to ask yourself that will help you manage through future family interactions. These steps require you to be fully honest with yourself and dig deep into your motivations. I know this can be painful, but it is essential for you to do it to move through these events without issues. [13-1] I suggest keeping a log of the events that come up and their outcomes. Perfect to keep in your phone calendar. It may come in handy later. Taking the time to get organized will slow you down and reduce the probability that you will deal with the situation in an inappropriate manner.

Why am I engaging in this event?

Ask yourself what your **motivation** is for attending an event or interacting with your ex. Write down in your calendar entry what is motivating you to go to this event or engage in this behavior. If your answer sounds something like, "it is the right thing to do" and not "I want to go," then reconsider engaging in this event. Step back from the situation and kindly explain that you will not be able to make it. You should want to engage with your family, not feel obligated to engage.

How will my behavior impact others?

If you share children or friends with your ex you need to ask how your behavior will impact them. An example might be when your child is getting married. For your children there are so many decisions to be made when planning a wedding. Having divorced parents can be incredibly stressful for the children. Rest assured there will be situations and events that will make you uncomfortable but try and remember what is best for your children. There may be times when you wish you could simply hide from all the discomfort. You might have the urge to control parts of the experience, so you don't feel so uncomfortable.

This urge is completely understandable. Some situations are going to be more difficult than others. For example, getting put at the same table as your ex's family. However, the more you try to accommodate your child's needs the easier you are making the process for them. By asking them to do what makes you comfortable you are adding more stress. For this one day or one event think about how you can lessen the burden on them. Try and remember that this is their day, be it a wedding, graduation, or even a little league baseball game.

What support do I need to help me through this event?

Being at an event which may involve your ex, or others that you may be uncomfortable with is going to be difficult. You need to think of what actions, or people might lesson your anxiety in going to such an event. Who are the people in your life that can help support you. Maybe even being at the event with you to help and support you if things were to get stressful for you. The very last thing you want is to cause a scene.

You need to create a game plan with your confidantes to get the best support possible. Do you want to bring a friend to the event? Do you schedule a massage before or after the event? How can you best take care of yourself and your feelings so that you can enjoy the event.

Are there any unfinished feelings I need to attend to?

Think about whether there is any unfinished business between you and your ex that might make the situation challenging for you. Are you holding resentment against your ex that might impact your ability to make decisions around whether to attend an event or not? Say the birth of a grandchild, how do you manage going to see your grandchild without running into your ex, or if you do cross paths what is your plan to be able to deal with it in an unconfrontational manner?

Resentment makes your life and all your interaction with family more challenging. By working through this resentment, you will have more flexibility when deciding how you want to respond to unforeseen interaction with your ex.

Conclusion / Lessons Learned

- What's in the divorce decree will dictate the minimum number of activities which you might be responsible for, like alimony for example, or visitation rights if you have younger children.

- Like it or not you will have to interact with your ex more than you may think. You need to come to this realization, and it will be easier on you.

- It's going to be hard, but you will need to set ground rules that you can commit to following.

- If you have children, remember that interaction with your ex will affect them one way or the other. Positive experiences will be received well. Anything negative could put further strain on your relationship with them.

- Keep centered and try not to overreact to anything that might be thrown at you.

- Keep interactions to activities which involve your kids. If you don't have any kids, then interactions with your ex should be at a minimum.

- During your marriage. Keep a budget force everyone to abide by it, there is no alternative. Take the time to review each months spending with your spouse, and family if they are old enough. You both must be on the same page when it comes to managing your finances. This was a major mistake of mine, one that cost me more than I care to admit.

Chapter-XIV: The Importance of Fathers

As Margaret Mead, the eminent anthropologist, wrote seventy years ago: "Every known human society rests firmly on the learned nurturing behavior of men". Kids need their fathers, just as they need their mothers. It's a simple, children understand, want and need interaction with both their parents.

As mentioned before, our society has let our morality slip away from us. With the court system defaulting to the mother's side; in some cases, ignoring facts around the divorce that should warrant a different outcome. Repeatedly it's the father who gets put under attack, and ridiculed. There are people that suggested and would like you to believe that kids principally only need their mothers. Even in today's TV programs do they paint the father in the light of playing a buffoon or clown type character of today's modern family.

This is a wrong assumption to be starting with when you're a judge or mediator making life altering decisions about the fate of children in the divorce. Many fathers who have been handed unfair settlements and have limited contact after the divorce, loved and wanted nothing more than to be involved in the children's lives. If you have never been a father, you can't even imagine how devastating this can be. To this day, I get emotional whenever people bring up things about their own children.

"It is scientifically and psychologically baseless, as well as a violation of human rights, to discriminate against men because of their sex in assignment of children's custody [or] adoption," according to American Psychological Association resolution [14-1]. As Kathryn Edin, a Princeton University sociologist and expert on low-income fathers, said: "If we truly believe in gender equity, then we must find a way to honor fathers' attempts to build relationships with their children just as we do mothers." [14-2].

Children Need Their Fathers

While fathers need and want their children in their lives, kids need and count on their dads even more. Unfortunately, this is where nasty divorces can damage a child's life. A divorce is between two adults it is no place to involve your children, especially if they are minors. Yet during this process, all too often spouses become incredibly angry at each other, so much that they want to punish the other at *ANY* cost. Not realizing that they could be damaging their own children by involving them in the details of your divorce.

Yet, no matter how hard you may try to come to a common ground with your spouse, they may not be thinking rationally. Despite all the expert advice and studies, the parent may still involve their children in the details of the divorce. Often the children become so enraged that they would never want to see the other parent again. There is no worse course of action for a parent to take than to push their children into having to choose between one parent or the other.

Fathers, as well as mothers, play an essential role in a child's development. Love and nurturing are important from both parents, but research demonstrates that father involvement positively affects their children's cognitive development, regulating their behavior, stimulating creative play, and developing their identity and social competence.

Even with divorced or unmarried parents who have split up, children who spend at least thirty-five percent of their time with each parent, rather than live with one and "visit" the other, have better relationships with both of their parents, while doing better academically, socially, and psychologically. There is an endless amount of data and studies that support the stance that children who don't have fathers regularly in their lives are worse off than those with fathers from childhood into adulthood [14-3].

These studies have shown that children typically feel abandoned, hurt, and angry. Boys lack good male role models and fail to develop, what NYU political scientist Lawrence Mead calls "the male virtues."

Children without fathers are twice as likely as other children to be treated for mental health issues. Thoughts of suicide are more common, approximately two-thirds of youth suicides occur among kids separated from their fathers. New boyfriends, or second marriage of their mothers can be supportive but are often new sources of conflict, especially for boys. This is a horrifying thought. Unless you're a professional who could even imagine such a statistic.

In school, children with little or no contact with their fathers are more likely to drop out of high school and roughly twice as likely to be suspended or expelled. We have the power to change this. As parents we need to put our differences aside for the sake of these innocent children.

Children also tend to score lower on standardized tests and receive lower grades. Strikingly, father absence may depress academic performance more than poverty does, as children from low-income, two-parent families outperform students from high-income, single-parent homes.

Children without fathers are about four times more likely to be poor, twice as likely to engage in criminal activity, and many times more likely to spend time in prison. Is this the future you want for your children? Stop being selfish and put the needs of your children ahead of your own.

Ninety percent of homeless and runaway children are from fatherless homes. Boys in mother-only households tend to be more aggressive and more likely to abuse drugs and alcohol, and almost three times as likely to carry guns and deal drugs. Nearly three-fourths of adolescent murderers grew up without fathers.

Girls, as well, are hurt when their fathers aren't around. Girls are more likely to be abused either by their parents, stepfather, or a mother's boyfriend. Daughters without fathers are more likely to be promiscuous, have children outside of marriage, have rocky relationships, and finally divorce. Wouldn't you do anything in your power to stop this wave of destructive behavior? Please parents, stop being selfish!

* The following statistics were reported by the United States Census Bureau. Published in Parents plus Kids

Other Shocking Statistics [14-4].

There are currently an estimated 72.2 million fathers in the United States
Breakdown of single fathers 44% divorced; 33% never married; 19% separated 4.2%widowed.
Children are four times more likely to be in poverty from a lack of a father in the home
Children living in a home without their birth father (24.7 million <33%>)
72.3 million Americans that think an absent father in the household is the most important problem facing American families
90% of runaway and homeless children are from fatherless homes *(National Institute of Justice)*
70% of minors housed in state facilities are from fatherless homes *(US Dep. Of Justice, 1988)*
Children without a father present are more likely to show disciplinary issues *(2017 US Census)*
Children in general, do better when their father or in some cases, a father figure, is in their lives
Kids with fathers who participate in their lives are more likely to do better in school than kids who don't have a father in the home *(US Dept. of Health & Human Services)*
Kids experience fewer behavior issues in school when a father figure is active in their life *(US Dept. of Health & Human Services)*
Boys get better grades in school when a father figure is in their life
Children in fatherless homes are twice as likely to be obese than children from a home with an active father figure
Children have a higher rate of drug and alcohol abuse in homes without a father

Lasting Impact

The harm done by having little contact with their fathers continues when they grow up. Comparing families of the same race and similar incomes, they are three times more likely to go to prison by the time they are 30. They are also less likely to be employed, according to Harvard economist Raj Chetty. Children without fathers in their lives create huge costs to society — not only in terms of poor academic achievement, but also mental-health problems, and criminality. The federal government spent about $100 billion dollars in taxpayer money to assist father-absent homes in 2006, a number that has steadily risen.

However, the most serious of the casualties of a divorce cannot be quantified. This is the emotional strain on the children. Sadly, some of it can be permanent. The most shameful part of this is it can all be avoided if the parents put down their selfish vindictive ways and come together to discuss what is best for their own children.

Please heed my pleas to not involve your children in your divorce details. Please try all means possible to keep open communications with your spouse when it comes to your children. Decide on a plan, so that your divorce from your spouse is only a divorce between you and your spouse. Do whatever it takes to keep the family together as far as the children are concerned.

Changing Fatherhood Stereotypes

For decades, the media portrayed dads as strong fatherly figures and good role models. TV shows had common themes of families coming together. Eating dinner together, having conversations, joking around, and being there for each other. In these sitcoms fathers were often made fun of but never really disrespected to the point that their value in the family was put in question. Families laughed together, cried together, and solved their problems together.

Fathers were wise, worthy of knowledge to be passed down to their children. They gave important life lessons. They had a strong presence in the family. Both father & mother worked as a team, sharing responsibilities, and took active roles in raising and discipling their children. There was none of this in my case, and that should have been a huge red flag to me. However, for whatever reason, I choose to ignore it. Abraham Lincoln stated, "a house divided against itself cannot stand," and that is still true today.

The TV of today does little to strengthen or even support the values of the role's fathers play in the real world. In an attempt at humor, the networks offered up the role of the father as a sacrifice. All of what a father truly represents is used in the opposite light. Before we knew what was happening, fathers were suddenly depicted as simpletons with no street smart or common sense, and only capable of making poor decisions. They are passive when it comes to disciplining their kids and being engaged in their family life. They are always caught confused and unaware of what is going on in their own families. The network's raced toward ratings, and the hell with preserving family values.

We live in what can often be a cruel world, the Jetson's are not our neighbors. Parents which are sole providers for their families, work all day long, doing whatever it takes to keep their family safe and happy. We rush home so we can get to our kid's events in time. We protect them with any means possible. Where are these lessons supported in the media and television of today? Where will our young men learn the real meaning of being a good father? Our children need role models that they can look up to and aspire to be like. Why must the media twist these relationships? All to be funny? Is it worth the damage they are doing to the next generations of parents, just for the sake of better ratings? Why can't it be a positive experience like it used to be for when my generation was growing up?

Conclusion / Lessons Learned

- I know I don't need to remind you that the children would not exist if it weren't for both of you.

- Your marriage is over, or soon will be, but never let anything get between you and your kids.

- Your kids need you more than ever before. Remember this when you encounter your ex, and you start to get stressed out.

- Don't sweat the small stuff, enjoy the time you have with your kids, as much as you can.

- If your situation is like mine, your relationship with your children might have been damaged by the process, false accusations, and fake stories. In these cases, it's going to take time for relations to open up again. It may go unnoticed but regardless, be there for your children whenever you are given the chance.

Chapter-XV: Dealing with the Aftermath

I must say that for me, divorce was the most stressful time of my entire life. It was a constant barrage of attacks and accusations which were physically and mentally exhausting. I had to sit ideally by and watch as I was found guilty of things that I had no idea even existed, let alone commit. I had to live with the frustration of watching my spouse play these games for her personal gain. She had no regard to the devastating damage she was causing to our children, family and friends.

I guarantee that you too will be exhausted from the process. As fathers we are expected to take care of everything, protect and provide for the family. We are expected to solve everyone's problems with unwavering dedication. Society paints the picture of men in general as unemotional, and if we do happen to show emotion it is taken as a sign of weakness. These are some of the reasons that divorce can have a prolonged lasting impact on the father more so than the mother. Many men hold their emotions in check, store them deep down inside of themselves so that they do not have to deal with them. However, these feelings don't simply fade away. They build up in intensity, just waiting to explode.

Professionals agree that it's a very serious issue that not dealing with the effects of your divorce are potentially very damaging to one's mental health. Even though there are studies which show that many men end up better off financially down the road, after their divorce, other studies show that divorced men have a higher rate of suicide [16-1] and are prone to alcoholism, weight gain, and mental health issues. Men's suicide rate is 4x times more often than divorced women. These are staggering statistics which cannot be and should not be ignored.

The research shows that one possible reason for this, is that divorced men lose their stable social standing and ties with society. Women, on the contrary, have more social support from family and friends and we have already seen, even the legal system has more support for the wife and mother.

Now think about what it feels like to have your children taken away from you by the courts, or limit visitation rights to only a few days a week or month. Then think about the impact of having your children turn against you for things that never happened or that were exaggerated during the divorce process. These all can be overwhelming with seemingly no end in sight. Sometimes the only answers can seem like the wrong answers. Be patient and impact what you can at any given time. Some things need time to settle before they can be addressed. There is no universal divorce playbook, no miracle cures for mental disorders.

Divorce from a Man's Perspective

Differences between men and women in relationships, creates the framework during and after the divorce, why the woman gets more empathy from those around her than the man. She has a stronger support network of relatives and friends who rush in to help and console her, and in unison, scold and ridicule her ex-spouse for their mistakes that led to the divorce.

Society tends to defend the women and assumes the break-up is the man's fault. Don't get me wrong – there are cases where this attitude is justified, maybe the father was a deadbeat dad, or abusive person. Yet there are countless more good men, and good fathers out there that are suffering from these prejudices.

Too many good fathers won't get to see their children grow up, because the courts give custody of the children to the mother and only a very small, limited portion of time to the father. For us who are lucky enough to have been paying for most of the household bills, we are rewarded with a large chunk of alimony and child support. Which drains our accounts and handcuffs our ability to get back to a normal financial life. I just think that the settlements being dished out should be a little more balanced, especially when it comes to the sharing responsibilities of the children. It's not about the money, its about the irreputable damage to the children which is the real crime here.

Emotional Stress

I'm not saying that women do not go through emotional stress and men do. However, society reinforces for many of us our upbringing that men don't show our emotional stress; "Men don't cry!". Men are taught to suppress these feelings.

The strong, silent type has been a manly ideal for a long time, embodied by the likes of Clint Eastwood, James Bond and who could forget John Wayne characters. Tough and stoic, their lack of emotional expression has long been a hallmark of traditional masculinity. Whereas girls tend to express their emotions more openly, boys learn that sharing their feelings is less than manly [16-2].

Research indicates, in contrast to the display rules for girls' emotions, boys are expected to show less of the "tender" emotions, such as sadness and anxiety and they are allowed to express externalizing emotions including anger, contempt and disgust. Anger and contempt function to promote the goal of overcoming obstacles, which can involve the pushing outward, rather than internalizing, of distress [16-3,4]. Thus, externalizing emotional expressions are consistent with societal gender roles for males to be assertive, individualistic, independent, and even aggressive, in line with traditional roles for men to protect their families and to overcome dangers that interfere with their ability to provide for their families [16-5,6].

Research also shows that holding back these emotions, or trying to bury them deep within us, are potentially extremely self-destructive. Creating quite the dilemma, and internal battle that fathers go through daily. While women can openly connect with others in their support networks, men often skip the grieving process altogether. They also seek professional help less often, thus losing a chance to improve their emotional state.

After divorce, men's emotions often include disappointment, shame, and regret, although many are disguised as anger and even rage. This is because these emotions are "acceptable" in society for a man's role model. This is why so many men struggle to keep their sanity after divorce.

Financial Hardship

Undoubtedly, it is much easier for a man with a high income to cope with paying for child support. For many ex-husbands, financial obligations to children and the former spouse may become a heavy financial burden. Even though you have split from your ex-spouse it does not break you away from your responsibilities as a parent for the children which the two of you brought into this world. At least until they are no longer minors.

This can be a financial challenge if in your circumstances you were just getting by making the monthly bills before the divorce. Now you no longer will be living with your ex-spouse, but you still must support your children. Child support is paid to meet the basic needs of the child, such as food, clothing, medical care, housing, and other necessities. While alimony is spousal support meant to allow spouses to maintain a certain standard of living. This may force you into renting rather than buying a house in the future. The additional expense of living in a new residence yourself adds to the stress tied to your circumstances post-divorce. Most likely, you will be forced to downsize your lifestyle as well. At least until you clear most of your outstanding debt and can establish a new baseline towards financial stability.

Changes in a Man's Behavior

The psychology of a divorced man right after their marriage breakdown may differ from what they usually feel or do. Some men who are going through a divorce can display changes in their behavior.

These changes are associated with the pain of losing their family and the need to rebuild their life. A common theme across numerous studies point to several tendencies which men turn to in trying to deal with the post-divorce pain.

He turns all his time to work - Men need to feel that they are worth something. For some, the only way to cope with it is to invest more time and energy in their careers. Hard work often brings tangible results and praise, which they lack in their new single life.

He turns to other releases - It can happen if a man skips the grieving process and tries to relieve the pain by doing all sorts of harmful things - parties, alcohol, promiscuous relationships. Fortunately, after a few weeks of such a life, most people taking this path come to their senses, while others continue down this dangerous road.

He won't let go of his pre-divorce life - Some men spend their free time stalking their exes, breaking into their social accounts, or blackmailing them. Such behavior prevents them from moving forward with their new lives and new relationships. I have real trouble with this one, being in the same state with my ex is not being far enough away from her for me. This is one post-divorce stress which I have nothing to worry about engaging in.

Social Isolation

Based on the numerous cases and situations previously mentioned, divorce for the man often signifies the loss of social connections and alienation. It's not rare when one partner "lures" all the mutual friends over to their side, and the other is left alone. This lack of family, reductions of social contacts, or a move to another location decreases the social support that will be available to one person over the other.

Lacking the social support and facing situations and emotions which are new to them is difficult for men to deal with. Rarely do men seek professional help from psychotherapists after the divorce. They try to cope with various emotions on their own, such attempts often are unsuccessful and can worsen their emotional balance.

For the men that are already dealing with anxiety, depression and stress these additional pressures can push them to their breaking point. For myself, having to deal with my ADHD and Bipolar disorder were challenging enough. During the divorce I chose to leave the house before the final decree, as living in the same house with my spouse was becoming increasingly difficult. My kids were clearly being turned against me, no one was talking to me; and with the winter months upon us, I was living in isolation. Leaving my house, children and close friend Echo, the family dog, was one of the hardest things I had ever had to do. I really had no alternative. I even left late on the evening of January 25th, nearing midnight. I could not even say goodbye to our dog.

It was ripping my heart out. My kids were changing, slipping away from me. My spouse was fabricating new accusations on a daily basis, which caused more lawyer activity, which drove up our legal fees. Her antics doubled the final costs of the divorce. Driving up costs was my spouse's plan from the beginning. She would like nothing more to bankrupt me. Leave me in so much debt that I could not recover, but just enough that I would have to maintain my job in order to keep her checks rolling in. At one point I'm sure she was being convinced by her supporting entourage that I would also be saddled with all the legal costs, hers and mine!

Even though I was left with more debt than many people have before they have declared bankruptcy, I wouldn't give them the satisfaction. One bright spot was that the mediator decreed that each of us was responsible for their own legal expenses. I know this was a shock to her, as until this time, most everyone, except myself and my lawyer, believed all of her lies and stories. At least all of her legal entourage became her responsibility to pay for. Pardon me if I do not shed a tear for her, knowing that her legal costs probably exceeded thirty thousand dollars. Rumor has it that even after getting a settlement of almost three quarters of a million dollars she didn't want to pay her legal bill when she saw the final price tag. I guess she could not talk her way out of that responsibility.

The Scars Left Behind

Even though leaving the house was very emotional I had to figure out where I was going to go to live. I could barely afford all the bills as it was. How was I going to afford renting a place on top of all of that? I could not even entertain the idea of imposing on anyone I knew.

After almost forty years the only option I had left was to move back in with my parents, some 1,200 miles away, in a land that defies aging; The Villages, Florida. I left my five thousand square foot house, the house which I poured my heart and soul into, the house I thought I would retire in, have my grandchildren visit me. Instead I moved back in with my parents. Yep, I was the proud owner of a 10'x12' bedroom, with a small window. Did I know what I was getting into? Absolutely, but what alternatives did I have? I really had no money to speak of to be able to afford my own place. Not even being able to rent a small apartment.

This is one area of my life of that I am ashamed of. Over the years, my spouse never wanted to make any time to visit my parents. In a twenty-year span never once did she want to go down to Florida to visit with them. Never once did we take the kids to visit them. They had come up to us for holidays and some family events over the years, but not once during the entire marriage did, we go to visit them. I should have known there was something very wrong with that. I managed to squeeze in a few visits on my own to visit with them for three or four days. But anytime I tried to bring up the subject of visiting with them as a family, my spouse would always have a laundry list of excuses that in the end prevented us from making the trip down to Florida. Ask me if we ever missed one of her family members occasions which involved visiting her parents ninety miles away in Long Island, New York. There would be an all-out war of an argument, whenever I suggested such a thing. If I were keeping score, I would say more than ninety percent of the time we would be hitting the road for a two plus hours traffic pact filled trip in each direction.

Even though I had reduced my personal belongings so that they fit into a small eleven by eleven bedroom, I was glad I was going to get time to spend with my 83+ year old parents. It was rare that I was able to take time off from work for family vacations, let alone time to visit my parents, and I'm truly embarrassed by it. I have relocated to their house for now, so I see them every day. I see how happy they are, having me living with them. My mom, now pretty much wheelchair bound, is thrilled to have me around. Especially, after having suffered through a stroke, two heart attacks, being paralyzed, not being able to speak and getting Covid while in the hospital, just a year prior to me coming down. It makes me sad and even angry that I allowed my parents to be treated the way that they were for all those years by my family. My spouse made it a habit of keeping the kids' conversation short whenever my parents would call them to see how things were going. No one ever knows how long any of us have left in our lives, but rest assured I'm making sure that I'm around for them.

You often hear people say that things happen for a reason, and that God only gives you what he knows you can manage. I won't argue that me moving down to Florida and in with my parents is not challenging at times, especially at the age of sixty, but I'm not embarrassed about living with them. If it wasn't for my parents, sister, and a handful of coworkers I would have had no one supporting me during this ordeal. I'm not sure I would have been able to have made it through to the end of the divorce proceedings without them.

Since moving to Florida, I have made some new friends, good caring and understanding people. I'm moving forward with my life one step at a time, but that isn't to say that I have my days where I feel overwhelmed, and lonely. Who wouldn't feel emotional knowing you're no longer welcome as a father. It's a challenge to keep focused during those times.

I find myself at times just sitting and staring at my bedroom mirror. A mirror where I have taped up pictures of my kids at all various ages. I have taped up on my mirror, old Father's Day cards, and birthday wishes that the kids have given me over the years. I have invitations and small pieces of artwork from my daughter that she created years long pasted, and copies of trophies that my son won during his little league baseball years with me as one of his teams' coaches. Having my children cut me out of their lives like I never existed is the worst feeling in the world. But NO ONE, can take away the memories I have, NO ONE can say these things never happened, or that I was not there for them. I'm the one that took all the countless hours of video from our family events, the birth of our children, the kids first birthdays, and numerous others. I will never be able to get past the damage my spouse caused because of her lies and character assassinations that she told my children. However long she lives, let her enjoy it, because for the rest of eternity she will not be able to change the facts that it was her greed and hatred that left our children with the scars that cannot be healed. It was her selfishness that changed the path that God set out for our children. I hope it haunts her for eternity, because nothing could make up for the time & relationships she has stolen from me with my children.

Conclusion / Lessons Learned

- Don't be ashamed, over 50% of all marriages will end in divorce.

- Divorce is hard, the longer it's drawn out, the more complicated it gets, the harder it becomes. Do not try and "tough it out,' and don't think that you can just wake up one day and your mental state will be unaffected. Seek out friends and family.

- Seek out professional help. There is no shame in admitting that you need help dealing with your emotions. Talking to someone about your feelings will give you a safe way to vent your anger, sadness, and pain.

- Not for one second should you start to doubt yourself about things that were mere accusations, fabrications, or incomplete bits of actions.

- In your quest for feeling "normal" again, put aside your attempts at short-term self-esteem boosting activities, as they are temporary and usually followed by the crash when you come back to earth and realize you still have the same emotional issues which you had previously.

- Allow yourself to move through the grieving process, if necessary, in the end you will come out with a new outlook and a new life, without your ex.

- Begin moving forward one step at a time. Don't rush into new relationships if you haven't recovered emotionally from your break-up.

- Fill your free time with self-development, new hobbies, and travel. New activities and a change of environment can help calm your nerves and get rid of negative thoughts.

- If you have children, take every opportunity to let them know how you feel about them. If you have been split apart from them, you will just need to work that much harder to get them back, forge a new relationship whenever the opportunity presents itself, just be there for them.

- None of these things will make a difference if the person is not ready to let go of the past. The main ingredient for recovery is the desire and the intention to start afresh.

Chapter-XVI: If Today was your Last Day

Don't squander this opportunity to have a fresh start! These words from this Nickleback song really resonated with me.

My best friend gave me the best advice
He said, "Each day's a gift and not a given right
Leave no stone unturned, leave your fears behind
And try to take the path less traveled by
That first step you take is the longest stride"

What if, if today was your last day
And tomorrow was too late
Could you say goodbye to yesterday?
Would you, live each moment like your last?
Leave old pictures in the past?
Donate every dime you have?
Would you, if today was your last day

What if, if today was your last day
Against the grain should be a way of life
What's worth the prize is always worth the fight
Every second counts 'cause there's no second try
So live like you'll never live it twice
Don't take the free ride in your own life

What if, if today was your last day
And tomorrow was too late
Could you say goodbye to yesterday?
Would you, live each moment like your last?
Leave old pictures in the past?
Donate every dime you have?

Would you, call old friends you never see?
Reminisce old memories?
Would you forgive your enemies?
Would you, find that one you're dreaming of?
Swear up and down to God above
that you finally fall in love?
If today was your last day

If today was your last day
Would you make your mark by mending a broken heart?
You know it's never too late to shoot for the stars
Regardless of who you are
So do whatever it takes
'Cause you can't rewind a moment in this life
Let nothing stand in your way
'Cause the hands of time are never on your side
If today was your last day

If today was your last day
And tomorrow was too late
Could you say goodbye to yesterday?
Would you live each moment like your last?
Leave old pictures in the past?
Donate every dime you have?

If today was your last day
(Nickleback)

There are no Do-overs

Until the invention of social media and on-line gaming, most of us as children got together with our friends outside or went over each other's house or apartment. Maybe we played tag outside, maybe some wiffle ball, kick the can (yes that was a real game in the 70's), kick ball in the school yard, and even Monopoly, if we had a few hours to kill during a rainy day. At some point during that time, something happened, a freak event, a distraction, a "time out" was maybe called. Then, someone shouted …"Do-Over"!

Shouting out "Do-Over" got the attention of everyone playing. It was a universal call to arms. It stopped everything in its tracks. At that point it was like a bunch of football referees getting together to watch the instant replay. However, out on the street corner, in the school yard, or even in the living room, there was no instant replay. The banter of what happened began, and like a court trial, the evidence was reviewed, parties came forward to recall what just happened. Then when everyone calmed down, the call was made to honor the Do-Over or not. In my neighborhood we had two honest kids that were always hanging with "the guys," which would include the girls as well. During which time we could not come to an agreement, someone would call out for "Wilson or Kulkain"! When these two spoke it was like law, they always called it like they saw it and were fair and impartial. They would make the call, and the activities would resume.

Then as we grew older, we grew out of a lot of those games we played as kids, but we continued with our favorites. Who does not remember playing any board game which involved dice? What happened when a die hit the board but bounced to the ground? Was that still a legal roll? I would wager that at least one person would shout out "Do-over"!

Fast forward a few decades. I'm playing golf with some new friends I have met in Florida. There is always a situation where someone skulls a drive into the water, or slices one so far to the side it bounces off a near-by house, what do we hear? I'm taking my "mulligan"! I'm talking about the average age is probably 75+, down in The Villages, Florida and they call me the "youngin" at 61! Well, in short a "mulligan" for those of you who are not familiar with the term, in its simplicity, is a "Do-Over."

Point being the Do-over has survived the test of time, we have leveraged it repeatedly throughout our lifetime. The Do-over had one weakness, it could never turn back time. Circumstances have changed, time has passed which we are never getting back. We need to recognize this, embrace it, and take advantage of it.

A Fresh Start

The fact is we all only have a certain amount of time before our mortality comes calling. There is nothing that we can do about that. However, there is something we can do about how we spend that time. We don't get to redo our life, and to be honest I wouldn't want to, nor would I want to forget the past, at least most of it! But I do want to move forward and start living my life. The bright side of a divorce is it gives us an opportunity to make a fresh start for ourselves.

From a divorce perspective, starting a new, doesn't mean walking away from our family, our children, it does mean leaving our ex-spouse behind and moving forward, making ourselves better. Taking advantage of the newfound time afforded us after the divorce is final, should be spent on improving who we are, or for some of us, finding ourselves.

When Steve Jobs was asked about this, his reply was …. "If you live each day as if it were your last, someday you'll be right.

Every morning I looked in the mirror and asked myself: If today were the last day of my life, would I want to do what I do today?"

When you think of all the meaningless things people do, you want to stop and ask them, "if today was your last day, what would you do?" What would you say if someone asked you that question? Would you do something different? Would you change your outlook on life, would you change how you treat each day? These are the questions you need to answer honestly. It all depends on where you are in life. The situation each of us lives with each day shapes how we live that day, and the next.

I came across a situation where I thought I was facing my own mortality. All I could think about was my children, and that I would never get to see them happy again, I would not be able to be part of their lives, I would not be able to help them when they might need it the most. There were many a night where I could not contain my emotions and just had so many things that I wanted to be able to do before it was my time. Then I got great news from the doctors that there was nothing I had to worry about. It took a while to get those feelings out of my head.

Don't Waste This Gift

I have trouble when talking with or having to deal with people who just don't think that they have been given a great gift and a great opportunity to do good for themselves and more importantly, good for others. It makes me crazy when I see people who are walking through life, just wasting the time they have on stupid things. They are making themselves miserable over things that they may not be able to change nor control. Things like:

- Arguing over small insignificant things with others. Things that don't matter if they go in one direction or the other. Think about, do you really want to be wasting your time arguing if cereal is better for you than Oatmeal? Come on people, let's get real here!

- Or people worrying about things that might, and statistically will never happen, instead of dealing with things that are happening. You all know those types of people. People that won't leave their house because they might be killed by a crossing bus. Should I even mention how I just love "doomsday preppers"?

- Or people that get into fights over nothing. Like the people that give into their anxiety during a tough commute and have a bout with a little road rage.

- People that wish bad things on others, so they can feel better about themselves let rage and hatred take over, instead of doing something nice for the people around them. More people should be focused on doing good things for others, making things better. Be generally happy for people rather than being jealous of what others might have!

- Finally, maybe the worse group of people that there is, are the people who have given up on life, stopped enjoying their lives. God gave us one life. We should try and not waste any of it. If you find yourself lonely, or physically alone, there are things you can do about it, and people you can talk with.

One thing you can control is how you spend your time. Please try and give back to others. You may not think your life has been interesting, but I assure you that it has. Get involved with a group that have similar interests as you do. Never just give up!

Make a Difference

Give your life a purpose beyond making money, saving for a vacation or retirement. I mean give your life a purpose in helping others in some way which allows them to move forward in live with a little less stress, a little less worrying and a little more hope than they had yesterday. Do this and I assure you that your life will be enriched as well.

As life would have it, we experience some tough times throughout our lives. We all remember how that felt. We also remember if we had to struggle through it alone, or did someone, somehow, someway, help us through it. It is during these times where even the smallest gesture can make an enormous difference to a person.

It is these moments that can give another person hope or make them forget about their problems for even a few minutes. It can break the chain of negativity that exists for so many of us. Each little change, each improvement can add up, they could even change the world if given the chance.

In one form or another I think I can say I have lived my life under the premise of making things better than when I found them. This could mean turning a parcel of land from a waste area to a beautiful garden, brightening the day for others who may follow. It could mean taking the time to simple listen to someone else's problems. Be empathetic to people's situations, have some compassion as to what they are going through. One day you may be that very person looking for help. Many of you have recently experienced a divorce, I shouldn't have to tell you about how difficult that has been on you.

Thank You for Serving

If it is one thing that I'm passionate about is thanking the people that go about their everyday lives helping other people. My heart goes out to every one of them. The first is the brave men and women of the armed forces. It doesn't matter what your political association is, no one can argue the fact that these men and women live their lives serving our country. They stand guard to protect our way of life. For all too many, they pay the ultimate price, sacrificing their own lives in defending our way of life. They shield us from the evils of the world. They do it with dedication and pride, they do it without question or hesitation. I thank every man and woman who have served and their families for the sacrifice they make so that we can enjoy our lives so freely as we do.

To those who serve our infrastructure, the police, firefights, and rescue crews, I thank you. These folks put others in front of themselves every day. They protect us while we sleep, they rescue us when we are in trouble. They do not just do this because it's their job or for the pension, they do it because they feel compelled to. They do this because they are driven to help others. We all need to remember this. Next time you see one of these providers, take the time to say thank you for your service. Offer to buy them a cup of coffee or take care of their lunch for them. It's a small gesture which can have a large impact.

Thanks, to the volunteers working with the homeless in the upper United States during the winter months to help make sure people can find shelter from the bitter cold. To the volunteers who donate their time to shelters that support people who have trouble getting through each day. For these volunteers they fight a never-ending battle. There are more people suffering through similar situations than we care to admit.

Don't turn a blind eye to the shelters that could use a few extra dollars or benefit from a few of your donated hours from your spare time. Even a few hours per month can make a tremendous difference to these shelters. You have the power to have influence in people's lives. I guarantee, you will feel better about yourself if you do.

I would be remiss if I did not thank all the teachers which help our children learn and grow. Many of the younger children look up to their teachers. Teachers take the time to make learning fun for these children. As our children get older, our teachers become role models. People we can tell our problems to, and guidance counselors who can help shape our future careers.

To this day I remember the teachers who helped me during that time of my life. My 11th grade science teacher who challenged me to push further and challenged me and my love of the sciences. My college computer science professors pushed me to realize if you want to advance further than most in your professional career, you must put in the time and be willing to sacrifice, to reach your goals.

Then there was my 10th grade math teacher, Mr. Busiello, he helped me recognize that every action has an impact on ourselves and the people around us. In my case it was a single event, an altercation with one of the kids on the football team, not too smart on my part. Mr. Busiello quickly made clear his position on interrupting his class and moreover, his position on fighting in his class. Now I will say his methods would not be acceptable by today's guidelines, but I will say they did get my immediate attention at that time. He took the time to explain to me what the consequences could be for my actions, if I continued to let others distract me in school. It really helped me. I will say, I still have a bit of a fear for school hallways. I also never interrupted another class for the rest of my high school years.

If you have children who are still in school, and you have not already, considered volunteering. Depending on how old your kids are, their teachers could always use your help. Instructing our young students is always a challenge, and they can always use an extra set of hands, or pair of eyes to keep a watch over the kids. The teachers will really appreciate any time you can give.

Take a day or even just a part of your day from work to help your kids class out. First off, I know you will feel good that you helped, and second, it provides another opportunity for you to interact and bond with your children. In a time of divorce this will mean a lot more to your children then you realize. Take advantage of any opportunity that allows you to do things with your kids. They will remember it for a long time, no matter how young or old they are.

Conclusion / Lessons Learned

- It's never too late to reach out to old friends. It's natural to be embarrassed or even ashamed that you have lost touch with good friends from your past.

- It's never too late to do something about regrets you may have about your life. As Nike would say, "just do it."!

- Cherish the times you have with your loved ones.

- Please remember to pay it forward. We are all fortunate, we have been granted the gift of life and we need to remember that.

- Don't be cheap, each one of us have a lot to offer others out there. You could be the one that makes that connection with someone that helps them turn their lives around.

- We all have the power to change the world. It may seem like we don't, but one small change, one improvement, one turn-around story makes a big difference if we all participate. Be different then you may have been up to this point. Start by trying to make a small difference in someone else's life.

Chapter-XVII: Given a Second Chance

I hope you have found this information beneficial to your circumstances and has given you some guidance in getting through a divorce and improving your life along the way and into the future. Even though my experiences may be different then your own, the experiences has hopefully shown you with any feelings of despair that you may be having. You are not alone, there are other folks who are experiencing similar circumstances and having similar feelings. It's common to feel like you are alone and have no one to turn to. It is during these times where you should not get discouraged. Don't hesitant to reach out to people in your network for support, this includes your lawyer(s).

Remember the end state of every divorce; is to get to the finish line. Divorce gives us a chance to build new relationships. This doesn't mean that you should forget about your past relationships. In most divorces there are relationships which have been damaged in some shape or form. The most important of these would be relationships with your children. Many children suppress their feelings. It's up to you to take the time to have discussions with them, comfort them to assure them that you will be there for them. Be patient, it's going to take time to mend these relationships.

You need to remember that this was your divorce and not theirs. If you were fortunate to be in a situation where your spouse and you were amicable with each other during the divorce the impact to the children will be minimized. Unfortunately, many divorces take a negative turn along the way. The uglier the divorce, the more challenging the mending process can be. Your spouse can be working against you in this healing process.

Your spouse can be feeding your children their version of what happened which may be a fabricated view of the truth. This was the situation I found myself in, and still find myself after a year the divorce was finalized. My children were greatly affected and they pretty much blamed myself for everything that happened leading up to and after the divorce was finalized.

As I sit here writing this, my children have not spoken to me since midway through the divorce, June of 2022, nor sent me any texts or emails. Even though they have purged me from their lives based on so many lies they were told, I'm not giving up hope for reconciliation in the future. We have had so many great memories over the years, and I think about them all of the time.

This may be near the end of this book, but it's not going to define the remaining chapters of my life. I have not forgotten; I have not given up hope that one day my children and I will have the chance to once again be together. A chance to laugh, as we so often did. A day to move forward and start building new memories. I'm still very emotional when I even think of my children, I always will be. It hurts me to know the pain they had to endure throughout these past few years, it was just so unnecessary.

They will always be welcome in my house. I hope, pray, and dream that one day there will be a knock on my door, and they will be on the other side.

It's a New Day

There will come a day when your divorce will be final and the dust will have settled. The stress and endless sleepless nights will be behind you. It takes tremendous strength and fortitude to get out of a marriage, but you did it. You have probably found a new place to call home. It might be in another town or even another state. No matter where it is, it's time to start your new life. You deserve it.

Sure, it will be a lot different at first. Depending on if you have minor children or not, will dictate the amount of alone time you have in the future. Going from a house full of other folks' activities to only having to worry about taking care of yourself will be quite the contrast. However, this is not necessarily a bad thing. Having this quiet time will allow you to think at your own pace, to gather your thoughts around how you will spend your time. What do you want to accomplish this time around? You will quickly come to realize that a whole new world has been revealed. Why would God send us down this new path if it didn't have purpose.

Think about it, you will be able to shape your life in any direction that you want. Do things that you always wanted to do, or that you haven't done for a long time. You will be able to hook up with friends which you have lost touch with. You will meet new people, people that may be looking for someone to help them get through similar difficulties.

In my case I had spent the entire year before the divorce rebuilding the outside of my house, you name it I was replacing or fixing it. I probably spent a thousand hours working on the house so that it would be in a better condition to sell. Think about having one thousand hours freed up in your calendar, it's liberating.

For me I got back to playing the game I loved, golf. I had barely played for over a decade as it was an expense I could no longer afford. Since I moved to Florida to be with my parents the bad weather was no longer an issue. It is sunny almost every day, and I look forward to playing golf on them Over those last few years of my marriage, I put on fifteen-twenty pounds on top of already being overweight.

Now that I was finally divorced, I have refocused my energy on living healthy, physically and mentally. I seem to have inspired people that I barely know, to want to also get healthy. For the first time that I can remember I'm starting to feel better about myself, I'm not hiding from the mirrors in the house. I can look in a mirror and not feel depressed and ashamed about my body. I try to make progress every day. I've now lost over forty pounds and six inches off my waist. I'm proud of my accomplishments and I'm excited about what I may find hidden around the next corner.

I want to Know What Love Is,

I've gotta take a little time,
A little time to think things over
I better read between the lines,
In case I need it when I'm older

> Now this mountain I must climb,
> Feels like the world upon my shoulders
> Through the clouds, I see love shine,
> It keeps me warm as life grows colder

In my life, there's been heartache and pain
I don't know if I can face it again
Can't stop now, I've traveled so far,
To change this lonely life

> I wanna know what love is, I want you to show me
> I wanna feel what love is, I know you can show me

I'm gonna take a little time
A little time to look around me
I've got nowhere left to hide
It looks like love has finally found me

> In my life, there's been heartache and pain
> I don't know if I can face it again
> I can't stop now, I've traveled so far,
> To change this lonely life

I wanna know what love is, I want you to show me
I wanna feel what love is, I know you can show me

> I wanna know what love is,
> I want you to show me
> I know you can show me
> Show me that it's real, our love, yeah

Foreigner

Relationships

It's funny about relationships, they can pop up without you even realizing it. I don't think there are many people that desire to be alone, it just happens. Science has proven that it's not healthy to be alone for extended periods of time. Forming new friendships is the healthiest thing that we can do.

We never know when a friendship could become a relationship. It will happen, there is no need to try and make it, or worse force it to happen. Friendships take time and so do relationships. You may have an instant attraction to someone you meet, but then as you spend time together, you may realize that you are two vastly different people, with little in common. Don't try and force fit the other person into being that perfect fit for you.

To me a relationship is a lot more than just a physical attraction. It's about finding that person that gets you for you. Finding that sole mate. The person you have similar interests with. The person that you are generally a happier person when you are with them. I think these are the makings of a healthy and sustaining relationship.

Coming out of a divorce we aren't always of right mind. We still will get stressed over things; we will feel pressure thinking we can't waste time. We want to 'check the boxes,' know that we have found that special person. Remember, you might run into that kindred spirit while in-line for your morning cup of coffee, shopping for groceries, or even playing a round of golf.

Relationships are funny, sometimes we may not even realize that we are in one, because it's so relaxed. There is no one that can tell you what a relationship is and how it should be defined. It's how do you define it. Sometimes we may not even want to admit to ourselves that we have found a special person in our lives, but if we really think about it, you will realize there is something special happening inside of you.

Coming out of a divorce we have too many things that remind us of and define what a bad relationship is all about, but do we even remember what makes up a good relationship?

- Being with a person who generally makes you smile and laugh. A person who when you are with makes you just feel like a calmer happier person. Finding yourself very relaxed and comfortable being with this person.

- Having that someone who you can be yourself around. This is not often an easy thing. Having that person who accepts you for you and doesn't try to change or "improve" you.

- You find yourself wanting to share your experiences with this person is a special relationship.

- Is this person someone who you think about often of when you are away from?

- Do you find yourself doing things that you know will make that person feel happy, and they do the same for you.

- Does this person put your concerns ahead of their own? A person who asks you about your day before they carry on talking about themselves.

- Are you comfortable cuddling up with?

- A person who you feel safe with when you are with them.

In my opinion these are some of the things that make a relationship special. If you find yourself thinking about the same person as you read this list, then you may want to hold onto that relationship because you have the makings of something really special.

Do not be discouraged if you don't have that perfect fit relationship at this point in your life. Continue to move forward, living your life, experiencing new things, the relationships will take care of themselves.

To My Oldest Son Austin

Austin means majestic dignity. It was a bright sunny day when Austin came into this world at 7 pounds 2 ounces and 20 inches long. It was a day that I will always remember.

Now, as Austin turned 31 years old, I remember the doctor saying, "here he comes," and seconds later, I saw him and the umbilical cord. I was a little nervous as his entire body was a tint of sky blue. No one ever told me that this is expected before babies take their first few breaths. I thought, how cool was that I just saw my sons first breaths in this world. A bit later when we were back in our room, they brought him in. He had such a calm sense over him. He wasn't crying, he was smiling. Like he knew everything was going to be alright, and that he could relax and begin his new life. Throughout his early years he was always smiling and never caused us any stress or headaches.

From as long as I can remember he was inventing things, building flying machines out of a bunch of pool floating noodles. Building forts and mazes by taking all the cushions off all the furniture, rearranging everything, covering cushions with sheets to make tunnels, and hiding places. He was always thinking mechanically.

There was almost nothing that would upset him. He is the definition of an old sole. Being an old soul means that you are wise beyond your years and mature for your age group, enlightened and smarter than other people of the same age. He gets along with any one he meets, regardless of their age.

He has compassion for any of god's creatures that are in trouble that he comes across. Not long ago, he was driving home from work late one night and saw a baby deer out of the corner of his eye on the side of the highway. He circled back and loaded a newborn baby deer into his car, as this little guy's mother was killed by a car a bit earlier and the baby wouldn't leave the mother's side. Hours later, I walked into the house and couldn't believe my eyes, but our husky was guarding this deer as he slept. The folks at work started calling him Deerrick. Well, Deerrick stayed with us for almost three weeks, the kids feed him milk and he even started eating some leaves from the plants in our yard. It's illegal to have a deer as a pet in Connecticut so after those three weeks we found Deerrick a home on a preserve in Upstate New York.

Austin and I also spent many a day and night during the late 90's and early 00's in the Bronx watching the New York Yankees. The family witnessed greatness when David Cone threw his perfect game in 1999. Austin and I also saw Aaron Boone's walk-off home run against the Red Sox's in 2003. It was that game where Austin realized that it was OK to yell out during the game. He was so excited yelling along with the other fifty thousand fans taunting the Red Sox players.

There were so many moments we had together. We went canoeing at a local park. It was especially fun because we really were never that good at catching fish. So much so that we would talk about what if this was the day, we would finally catch the big one.

Then there were countless times where we went paintballing together. Austin, his friends, and I, would head out at the break of dawn and not get back until much later that afternoon. I remember that I could barely walk the next day as we spent so many hours in the woods, stalking the other team. We really had a great time. There were so many moments to talk about.

The year I got Austin his first car, he, my dad, and myself did a full interior restoration together. My dad still talks about it to this day. We must have spent a few hundred hours sanding the interior panels, prepping them, taping them off. Then spraying and sealing them at least two or three times. The car looked spectacular, and Austin was so excited. The three of us really had a great time doing that project together.

We have had so many great times together, he and I, it was glorious. Times that no one can take away. They were so genuine. It upsets me beyond anything you can image, to have seen Austin be manipulated with lies, and accusations by his mother and other members of the family. So much that this mild mannered, brilliant young man, would never want to see me or talk to me again. Seeing the results of what he turned into by being convinced of things that never happened just broke my heart. It changed him inside.

He was beyond approach. Every time I tried to talk with him, his mother would be there behind closed doors to tell him more tails. I hope and pray that one day he will question some of these things. That one day, he will see that the facts as he was told, don't add up. That these stories were told to him to rob him of his memories of his father while inflicting as much pain as possible on me, regardless of the impact on Austin.

I hope and pray that there will be one day where I get to see him again, one day where we can remember all the great times we had. I pray for the day when we will be able to forget the lies and we will be able to make new memories together. I'm not even sure what I would say if I opened the door and saw him standing in front of me. I might just break down and cry with joy. I think maybe I would just ask him, how he's been. I would want to hear everything he has been up to over the years. I will always be just a phone call away. A short email if he wanted to say "hi, how you been."

There is not one day of my life which I do not think about him, I miss him so very much. I need him to know that I will always be here for him. He will always be my son.

To My Daughter Lindsay

Ever since you first started walking, I knew you were going to grow up as a leader. You had tremendous purpose and drive as you struggled to take your first steps. You were excited when you reached your destination. Especially if that destination was where your big brother Austin was playing. You always had to be with him.

Throughout your life you have always moved forward with determination, letting nothing get in your way from achieving your goals. Your inherent talents and vibrant personality brightened every room you entered. You impressed every teacher with your quest for knowledge and drive to continually push yourself to be better. There is an energy around you which is infectious. Every person you meet wants to be a part of your projects. You work in a high-pressure field that have seemingly impossible deadlines. Yet so many senior theatre professionals want you as their set designer. They turn to you for your imagination and innovative designs. They turn to you because they know that you will get the job done, no matter what it takes, and the results will be beyond their expectations.

You have grown into a beautiful and amazing young woman. I'm so very proud of you. Even though these last few years I have had to admire you and your work from a far, I still track your activities. I follow you and your career the best I can, through whatever avenue I can find. Thank God for social media. The productions which you have been a part of amaze me, you amaze me. You live your life with such humility and grace, your kind and caring. It is no wonder why you have been so successful. No father could be prouder of their daughter than I am of you.

I have been amazed at what you have been able to accomplish in such a short time. I still have some of your early works, like the invitations you made for our annual Easter Egg hunt for the neighborhood. The heart you made for school; it was so colorful. In it you had Mrs. Lynch your art teacher, your favorite things you liked to do, like writing, music, skiing in Vermont, your childhood friends, holidays, and right in the middle a big yellow star with your family all named.

Your writing has always been amazing, well beyond your years. You wrote your own short story at the age of 10, it was self-published. I will never forget it, it was called "Sleepover Problems." This book had fully illustrated the events of those two days. Each page a complete work of art, with great attention to detail, and yes, it was to scale and in full color. It also had the front and back cover laminated! You dedicated it to your friend Meghan Callan who lived only a few houses down the street. You always said that it allowed you to remember all the great times the two of you had together. It was not just a story of great times during a sleep over, it was also about the internal struggles you had, as it was your first sleep away from home. You described how Meghan and her mom helped you overcome your sadness. When I read it, I'm still amazed you were only ten when you wrote it.

Lindsay also made this beautiful butterfly, completely out of dozens of soda cans. We had it hanging in our kitchen. Then, when she entered Boston University, college of Fine Art, she continued producing outstanding results. Two such works hung in the Boston University art gallery while she attended. These were no small pieces; they were four by six feet canvases. One, a depiction of a popular New York city scene, where a woman was hanging out of a taxicab window kissing a man on a motorcycle. It just took my breath away. I later found out that during the showing an admirer bought the painting for one thousand dollars. I wish I would have known about this, because there is nothing, I would have given to have that painting on my wall today. One day I will find that painting and hopefully be able to convince the owner to sell it to me.

Another four by six canvas work was of a bright red apple with water bouncing off it. It was so real that you could just taste the apple and feel wet splashes as they bounced off the apple. This was one of my favorites, it was mounted prominently on the center of the wall in our living room. Unfortunately, I was unable to bring that painting with me when I left our house for the last time. I hope it found a new home on one of her walls.

If I ever have the chance to talk to her again, I will want to hear about everything that has happened in her life. Every show that she has been involved in, every piece of art that she has created, and everything in between. At the time she stopped all communications with me she was going with Blake, an amazing man, also involved in the theatre at night and computer tech during the day. They were the perfect fit for each other. I loved watching them prepare a meal together. They would put on some music; decide what specialty drink they would have during the preparation. Blake was not only kind and caring, but a complete gentleman. During Covid he came to live with us for over a year, and it was a wonderful time for all of us. He and Lindsay would do the simple things in life, like go on walks into the woods with our dog Echo, hang out by the pool and read together, and they even helped me hang Christmas lights. It was a real pleasure to watch.

I am confident they are still together, and I hope that one day I will hear all about their adventures. It is great to see them living life, and not letting life's complexities get the best of them. A lesson which took me almost sixty years to figure out. I am so happy for them, and so in awe of my daughter who I love with all my heart.

One day I hope that she and I will be able to have a relationship again, and maybe we can catch up on all the things which I have missed over the years. I hope one day that she will become comfortable asking me anything that might be bothering her. I will always be waiting here for her if she ever needs anything. I hope I'm given the opportunity to build back our relationship. She will always be my daughter.

To My Son Tyler

Tyler is an incredibly special young man. He is a very gentle, quiet, thoughtful, and a bit shy, young man. He never wants to draw attention to himself, even when he deserves the acknowledgement.

In December 2012, twenty children and six adult were fatally shot, in Sandy Hook, Connecticut. This occurred one year after Tyler had graduated from the school. He knew the adults and some of the children from his years at the school. It was extremely hard for Tyler for many years to follow. Tyler was afraid to leave the house, afraid to go out in public. Tyler and I would go bowling all the time, but after the attack we would make sure that we went during off hours when most people had gone. We had a great time together. It was exciting to watch Tyler bowl, he would throw it from the side of his body. I remember one game where he could barely miss. He threw a 267, amazing for a kid his age.

Tyler and I also loved playing one-on-one whiffle ball down on the ball field. I converted a section of woods in our backyard into a baseball diamond to scale for 10-12 year olds. The pitching mound was a perfect match. We had endless games on that field. I gave him a good battle, but in the end he won most of our games.

There are so many things that we did together that I will never forget. From an early age, Tyler had a tremendous talent for baseball. Part of me is saying this as a proud father, but the rest of me is saying this as a realist. Tyler was born to be a baseball pitcher. Starting from when he was only two, he would throw the baseball against the wall for hours on end. You could tell he just had a way about him, as he got older, he just loved to pitch and pitch and pitch, quite often until darkness set in.

I'll never forget the very first time he was asked if he wanted to pitch during a game. He was only 6-years old at the time. He did not like to be the center of attention, but he loved to pitch more than anything in the world, so he slowly went to the mound.

The dads decided that each batter could stay in the batter's box until they struck out swinging. I was catching for Tyler. He threw the first pitch for a strike as it made a pop into my catcher's glove. A few dads looked up, as well as the coaches. I looked at the batter and he took a little step backwards. There was not much of an arch to his pitches, he just reached back and fired another one, right down the middle. He threw the next five pitches right down the middle, popping the glove every time. Everyone was now watching, and he was not phased in the least. The batter only swung one time, and after more than twenty pitches, all for strikes. The coach called up the next batter. It was amazing to see this little boy, have such command of the game, his emotions, and his talent. As God as my witness, he threw over 30 pitches that inning before I said that was enough pitches for one day. He only threw three balls the entire time.

I will always cherish every time I saw him take the mound. I admired his courage, he would never back down from a batter, even when they were two or more years older than he was. He never shied away from a tough situation. Max, one of the coaches from an outside travel team, who had spent some time in the minor leagues, recruited him at the age of twelve. I remember one game where the entire pitching staff couldn't get the ball over the plate. I think there was 15 walks in the first four innings. Max called Tyler into the game, as Tyler left the mound after getting three outs on only five pitches Max said to him, "I just love watching you pitch. You just throw strikes and get outs. Pitching to contact that's what it's all about". Tyler just smiled in his humble manner.

I loved watching Tyler pitch more than anything. I never wanted to make Tyler nervous, which he never did in any case, so I would hide behind various things and peak around the corner. The other parents always got a kick out of it. I would be peaking around a tree, the visitors' dugout, a smelly port-a-potty. Nothing was going to stop me from watching him pitch. How he stayed so calm I will never know. Me? I was a nervous wreck just watching him. Nothing phased him, like I said he was born to pitch.

Then one early spring day in Connecticut, it was a cool morning. Tyler went through his usual warm-up and took the mound for the first inning. Midway through the inning he threw a pitch, latter saying he said he felt a pinch. The bases were loaded. I could see him nod to the coach that he was OK. He threw only one more pitch it was a come-backer line drive up the middle, he snagged the ball then threw to first base for the double play. Little did we know that was the last time he would throw a baseball in a live game. To this day whenever I think about this I immediately tear up.

He had to take 9-12 months off with no throwing, not one throw. Then he went into a rehab style workout over several months. It was so emotional for everyone. Knowing how much this young boy loved baseball. He knew he was good, incredibly good. It just broke my heart. For a few years he was nervous to throw hard to anyone but me. We would go to a local ball field to throw and hit. We had so much fun.

Even though he's twenty-two now, I know in my heart he could try again. I know he's still hesitant, but my faith tells me that he has what it takes. Maybe he doesn't "make it" but I pray every night for him that one day he would be able to pitch in a live game situation. Just so he could have that feeling again. Just so he knew that he fought back, against what others were saying, that he conquered the challenge, and won. I also hope that I would have the great pleasure to have a catch with him, and maybe even catch a few imaginary batters like we used to do so many, many times before. I still have my old beat-up glove in my closet in case he was ever to visit me in Florida.

Another thing we loved to do together was play PokemonGo. Austin collected Pokémon cards when he was little, but I never knew there was a mobile app until the summer of 2016, when I became an owner of my first Pokémon ("pocket monster"). People often thought it was a bit strange for a 50+ year old to be playing a "kids" game. I looked at it like an opportunity to spend more time with my son. As I learned the game, it was a lot of fun. We explored, in search of the rarest of Pokémon. We used to go all over town, like hunting for buried treasure. You would team up with other Pokémon trainers to defeat the largest and strongest of Pokémon. We would battle each other, trade with each other, it was great fun. We were always on the quest for a "shiny" Pokémon. One that was the rarest and was different in color than its non-shiny form. As the divorce proceeded, he deleted me as a friend in the game. I'm still an active player, I play in hopes that one day I will get a friend request from him. It would be nice to start to do the things that we loved so much to do before he was dragged into the divorce.

I'm happy to say that there are too many memories to mention here. Too many great, unforgettable memories. The one thing that I hope he realizes is how much I love him.

It pains me to know that the last time I saw him, he was threatening me with a baseball bat. He was filled with such hatred and sheer rage towards me. His mind was made up that I was somehow this evil person, this deadbeat father which he no longer wanted to be a part of his life.

I'm sorry that he got dragged into his parent's divorce. I never wanted that for him. He was told lies by his mother about things that never happened. Others misused their relationship with him to destroy the relationship we once had. One day I hope he gets to read this. I hope that one day I'll get to have him in my life again.

I will always love him with all my heart, I will always be there for him if he ever needs me. If he so desires, I will sit down with him and answer any questions he may have, for as long as it takes. I just hope I'm given that chance to set the record straight. I hope I'm given the chance to rebuild a relationship which was unjustly stolen from us. I welcome a time when I'll be able to have a catch with him. I miss him so much.

Epilogue

No one said life was going to be easy. There is no universal playbook for every situation we may find ourselves in. But I do know that we don't have to be alone during this journey. Life was never intended to be lived alone. However, throughout life we are challenged with situations which make us feel isolated and alone.

It was intended that we were put on this earth to help one another. To live life to its fullest, to not waste this gift which we have been given. We find ourselves having all kinds of relationships with many different types of people throughout our lifetime. We are fortunate when we can look back and say that a particular relationship has made a profound impact on our lives.

This is not to say that there is something wrong if we don't have such at relationship at this time. There are countless reasons why we may not, but that should not get us down. It's exciting at the opportunity to form new relationships. It's one more adventure, one more gift, that we get to experience. One more person we get to share things with.

Even though society labels marriage with the tag "till death do us part," did God intend us to waste a portion of our lives being miserable? Being trapped in a situation where we were wasting that precious gift that he gave us? I personal do not think so!

No one can argue that divorce does not bring uncertainty into our lives. Most people find it difficult to deal with change. But divorce also brings with it the hope of allowing each one of us to live life to its fullest. It allows us a chance to break away from difficult times and horrible situations. It gives us a chance to feel alive again.

We are all brought into this world the same way. However, once we take our first breath, each one of us will experience life in its own way. Each one of us will deal with similar situations differently. Each one of us is wired a little bit differently. Who is to say which is right and which is wrong. Some of us will thrive while others will struggle.

There is nothing that prevents us from questioning who we are, question why we are the way we are. If we were put on this earth to live life to its fullest, don't we owe it to ourselves to strive to improve? To question things that others may take for granted? To seek out ways to make challenge ourselves?

A lot of times we cannot go it alone, we need to accept the fact that we need help from others, just as we need to offer a helping hand to others who may need it. Our minds are made up of millions upon millions neurological connections. Those connections form our cognizant thoughts, how we act, how we perceive life. Today more than ever before, we are fortunate to have the knowledge and understanding of how our minds are wired. We have the capability to mend these connections which may be causing struggles with ordinary life's circumstances. Altering these connections allows for our mind to process at its intended capacity, more efficiently and effectively. Our mind is arguably the most important, most powerful organ in our body which controls thought, memory, emotions, touch, motor skills, vision, breathing, temperature, hunger, and every process that regulates our body. Together, the brain and the spinal cord makes up our central nervous system. Wouldn't each one of us want to make sure it is all working at its optimal levels?

Each one of us have the capability to break free of the situations that we may find ourselves in. Be it a failed marriage, stress and anxiety, loneliness, depression or something else. We are all born with the ability to adapt to change. You may be feeling trapped and alone at times, but don't let this define you, don't allow this to be the final chapter of your life.

Tomorrow morning when you wake up, look out at the sun rising and take a deep breath. Realize that this is a brand-new day. A day that you can take control how it affects you, it's a day that you can take back your life. It's up to you to write the next chapter in your life. You will be surprised at who you will may along the way, embrace it

Live, Love, and Share Life's Gift!

Keep Trying,

When things go wrong
And your dreams take flight,
And you feel like quitting
But you must fight-

When disappointments come
And you feel like crying,
And you want to run away
But you must keep trying-

Remember success
Means refusing to quit.
It means you try harder
When you're hardest hit.

Perry Tanksley
May the Lord bless and keep you Hum 6:24

Bibliography

[3-1] (15) Most Common Reasons Behind Lack of Intimacy in Marriage, Dec, 2023 Shannon McHugh, Psychologist / by Sylvia Smith

[3-2] What to Do if Your Relationship Lacks Physical Intimacy | Psychology Today, Sep, 2021   Deborah L. Davis Ph.D.

[3-3] What is Emotional Neglect in Marriage? Signs & How to Deal, Jan, 2024 Maggie Martinez, LCSW / by Sylvia Smith

[4-1] Mental Health Disorder Statistics, Mental and Behavioral Health, 2023; https://www.hopkinsmedicine.org/health/wellness-and-prevention/mental-health-disorder-statistics ,John Hopkins Medical Journal

[4-2] Mental Health, 2023 https://www.mayoclinic.org/healthy-lifestyle/adult-health/basics/mental-health/hlv-20049421 Mayo Clinic Staff

[4-3] Mental Disorders, Jun, 2022 https://www.who.int/news-room/fact-sheets/detail/mental-disorders by The World Health Organization website

[6-1] D'Onofrio B, Emery R. Parental divorce or separation and children's mental health. *World Psychiatry*. 2019;18(1):100–101. doi:10.1002/wps.20590

[6-2] The High-Conflict Divorce & Your Children's Adjustment, Jun 2011, Family Advocate, Chicago, Vol. 34, Iss. 1, pgs. 32-34 by Arnold T Shievold

[6-3] Family Advocate by Shienvold, pgs 32-34

[6-4] McWilliams, Family Advocate pgs 8-11

[6-5]   Protecting Your Children Before, During, and After Your Divorce, Jun 2018, Family Advocate, Chicago, Vol 41, Iss. 1, pgs. 8-11 by Joan H. McWilliams

[7-1]   Based on the research of Doctor Frank T. McAndrew Ph.D. posted in Psychology Today April 4th, 2022. Dr McAndrew is a professor of Psychology at Knox College

[7-2]   PsychCentral: Jan26, 2018 https://psychcentral.com/blog/relationship-corner/2018/01/female-vs-male-friendships by Tarra Bates-Duford, Ph.D., LMFT

[7-3]   Twelve-month and lifetime prevalence and lifetime morbid risk of anxiety and mood disorders in the United States. Int J Methods Psychiatr Res. 2012;21:169–184 by Kessler RC, Petukhova M, Sampson NA, Zaslavsky AM, Wittchen

[7-4]   The persistent and pervasive impact of being bullied in childhood and adolescence: implications for policy and practice. J Child Psychol Psychiatry. 2018;59:405–421 by Arseneault L. Annual research review:

[7-5] The risk of social isolation – American Psychological Association (APA);   http://www.apa.org/monitor/2019/05/ce-corner-isolation

[7-6] Social Isolation, loneliness in older people pose health risks; https://www.nia.nih.gov/news/social-isolation-loneliness-older-people-pose-health-risks

[7-7] How does lack of human interaction affect mental health? https://wellbeingport.com/how-does-lack-of -human interaction-affect-mental-health/

[7-8] The effects of social deprivation on adolescent development and mental health https://www.ncbi.nlm.nih.gov/pmc/articles/PMC7292584/

[7-9] Understanding the Effects of Social Isolation on Mental Health https://publichealth.tulane.edu/blog/effects-of-social-isolation-on-mental-health

[7-10] Lancet Child Adolesc Health. 2020 Aug; 4(8): 634–640. PMCID: PMC7292584;   Published online 2020 Jun 12. doi: 10.1016/S2352-4642(20)30186-3
        PMID: 32540024

[9-1] May T, Adesina I, McGillivray J, Rinehart NJ. Sex differences in neurodevelopmental disorders. *Curr Opin Neurol.* 2019

[9-2] Bale TL, Baram TZ, Brown AS, et al. Early life programming and neurodevelopmental disorders. *Biol Psychiatry.* 2010

[9-3] Masuda F, Nakajima S, Miyazaki T, et al. Clinical effectiveness of repetitive transcranial magnetic stimulation treatment in children and adolescents with neurodevelopmental disorders: A systematic review. *Autism.* 2019

[9-4] Kim YH. How can pediatricians treat neurodevelopmental disorders. Clin Exp Pediatr. 2021

[9-5] Levy SE, Hyman SL. Complementary and Alternative Medicine Treatments for Children with Autism Spectrum Disorders. Child and adolescent psychiatric clinics of North America. 2015.

[9-6] Mary Fetzer; ADHD Online Diagnosis & Treatment; Article October 31,2022; https://adhdonline.com/articles/29-famous-people-show-how-adhd-does-not-have-to-limit-success/

[9-7]   Family adjustment and interventions in neurodevelopmental 2015 disorders. *Curr Opin Psychiatry*. by Dykens EM.

[10-1] Bipolar Disorder, Feb, 2023, National Library of Medicine (NIH); https://www.ncbi.nlm.nih.gov/books/NBK558998/#:~:text=Bipol ar%20disorder%20is%20characterized%20by,response%20occur %2C%20particularly%20with%20depression. By Ankit Jain & Paroma Miltra

[10-2]   Mental Health Information: Bipolar Disorder, 2023 https://www.nimh.nih.gov/health/topics/bipolar-disorder Source: National Institute of Mental Health

[10-3] Northern Lakes, Community Mental Health Authority; https://www.northernlakescmh.org/learn/general-mental-health-topics/famous-people-who-have-had-a-mental-illness/. Source: National Alliance on Mental Illness (www.nami.org)

[10-4]   Marwaha S, Durrani A and Singh S. Employment outcomes in people with bipolar disorder: a systematic review. Acta Psychiatr Scand 2013 by Marwaha S, Durrani A and Singh S.

[10-5] WHO World Report on Disability: a review. Disabily Health J 2011 by Krahn GL

[10-6] Precision Medicine Center of Excellence in Mood Disorders, April 2023 John Hopkins University, Diagnosis and Management of Bipolar Disorders, BMJ by Fernando S Goes

[10-7] Prevalence and correlates of bipolar spectrum disorder in the world mental health survey initiative. Arch Gen Psychiatry.2011/Archgenpsychiatry 2011, by Merikangas KR, Jin R, He JP, et al.

[10-8] Prevalence of attention-deficit/hyperactivity disorder in people with mood disorders: A systematic review and meta-analysis. Acta Psychiatr Scand 2021 by Sandstrom A, Perroud N, Alda M, Uher R, Pavlova B.

[10-9] Institute of Health Metrics and Evaluation. Global Health Data Exchange (GHDx), May 2022; https://vizhub.healthdata.org/gbd-results/

[13-1] Psychology Today; Aug, 2022; https://www.psychologytoday.com/intl/blog/divorce-course/202008 by Elizabet Cohen, Ph.D.

[14-1] American Psychological Association. (Child Custody (apa.org), https://www.apa.org/about/policy/custody created 2008).

[14-2] Princeton University; Department of Sociology, Kathryn Edin, "Does Time with Dad in Childhood Pay off in Adolescence?" Journal of Marriage and Family. 82(5): 1587-1605.

[14-3] National Library of Medicine; National Center for Biotechnology Information. The Causal Effects of Father Absence - PMC (nih.gov)

[14-4] The Statistics Don't Lie: Fathers Matter, Jun 2023 National Fatherhood Initiative, https://www.fatherhood.org/father-absence-statistic, Data taken from the U.S. Census Bureay (2023)

[15-1] National Library of Medicine, Marital status and suicide in the National Longitudinal Mortality Study, Journal of Epidemiology & Community Health; 2000 Apr; 54(4): 254–261; http://dx.doi.org/10.1136/jech.54.4.254. Augustine J Kposowa, Department of Sociology, University of California

[15-2] Psychology Today, Why Bottling Up Emotions is Central to Masculinity, Lian Shira April 2nd 2016; https://www.psychologytoday.com/us/blog/the-narcissus-in-all-us/201604/

[15-3] Brody LR. Gender, emotion, and the family. Harvard University Press; Cambridge, MA: 1999. [Google Scholar]

[15-4] Brody LR, Hall JA. Gender and emotion in context. In: Lewis M, Haviland-Jones JM, Barrett LF, editors. Handbook of emotions. 3rd The Guilford Press; New York, NY: 2008. pp. 395–408.

[15-5] Brody Brody LR, Hall JA. Gender and emotion. In: Lewis M, Haviland JM, editors. Handbook of emotions. Guilford Press; New York, NY: 1993. pp. 447–460.

[15-6] Brody LR, Hall JA. Gender and emotion in context. In: Lewis M, Haviland-Jones JM, Barrett LF, editors. Handbook of emotions. 3rd The Guilford Press; New York, NY: 2008. pp. 395–408.

Acknowledgments

I want to thank my lawyer; she got me through some of the toughest times of my life. She was one of the few people who believed in me. She helped me understand the process, while navigating the mind field. I would be hard pressed to find another lawyer who would have put up with what Janise did. Janis wasn't just my lawyer; I now consider her friend.

Thanks, Janise, for Saving My Life

I want to thank my friends & coworkers Bhargava & Anoop who took the time out of their busy lives to listen to my struggles, while keeping me grounded. They were straight shooters during this ordeal. They kept me upbeat throughout the entire process.

*Thanks all for being
there for me*

Thanks to my mom & dad. Even though I didn't spend nearly enough time with them over the past 30 years, they tried to comfort me in any way that they could. Not always knowing what to say or how to help me, they stood by my side, when so many others turned against me. I know I can't replace for time lost, but I hope now being able to see them every day somehow makes it better for them.

*Thanks for never giving up on me.
Thanks for listening,
Love you so much!*

Thanks to my sister. She got the short end of the stick, and I let it happen. I'm truly sorry for that. Thanks for everything you've done for me these past few years, I'll never forget it.

Here's to a
lot more good times to come!!

Big thanks go out to my real second family, my friends at GE. You all know who you are. You are all amazing. The support and friendship that we have shared over my plus ten great years at GE have been a true inspiration to me. I can't thank everyone enough. Cheers to everyone, here's to "Making a World that Works!"

Thanks for putting up with all my long PowerPoints,
loud talking and crazy ideas
Good Luck to Everyone

About the Author

Michael Fuori grew up in a small town on Long Island, New York and showed a talent with computers at an early age. He became an entrepreneur at a young age. Building a small landscaping business which funded him through college.

Michael went to college at, Nassau Community College, where he carried a 4.0 average. Michael then transferred to Hofstra University where he completed his four years, graduating with a Bachelor of Science with a minor in accounting.

Michael was a published author before the age of 25, coauthoring "Introduction to Pascal Programming Language" and "Introduction to Fortran Programming Language". Michael went on to work at Chase Manhattan Bank as a junior COBOL programmer. After his day job was over, he went to work at a bar in Levittown New York that he had purchase shortly after starting his position at Chase. He then moved into a senior analyst position at Morgan Stanley. In 1995, he landed a job at IMRS, later to become Hyperion, then to be bought by the Oracle corporation.

Michael become one of the elite consultant in Financial Consolidations product suite with Hyperion. He left Hyperion and was hired by Warner Music Group. One year later he started his own Hyperion Consulting firm, Lindin Consulting. Then in 2002 merged companies to form Pinnacle where he was CFO & COO. He landed both companies on the Inc-500 fastest growing companies in America, as recognized by Inc Magazine. Michael has spoken at dozens of technical conferences as one of the leading subject matter experts in the field of Financial Consolidations for Hyperion EPM.

Despite the challenges he faced from his mental disorders, Michael & his partner, built Pinnacle into a fifty-person multimillion dollar firm. Later in 2008 they sold their consulting company. After spending a few years as an independent consultant, he settled down taking the lead role; Principal Data & Information Architect with the General Electric company, where he is still employed today.

Michael was married at the age of 28, has three lovely children, Austin, Lindsay, and Tyler. Michael was proud to be an assistant manager, then manager of his son Tyler's little league baseball team. At the age of fifty, Michael was diagnosed with having ADHD and being bipolar. After 30 plus years of marriage Michael and his wife Laura divorced in 2023.

Throughout his life, Michael loved solving puzzles. That fondness for puzzle solving transformed into his love of solving problems for his customers through custom software. Michael believes that if you worked hard enough, have no fear of failing, that there isn't any technical problem which can't be solved. He especially liked the challenge to make things process faster. He loved taking on the challenges where others had failed. Michael sets an extremely high standard for himself. Optimizing, creating, and building software solutions which deliver real value to his customers, is what drives Michael to the high levels of success he aspires to. Michael has been involved in several mentoring programs.

Michael loves Baseball, but enjoys all sports, rooting for the New York Yankees, Dallas Cowboys, and New York Rangers. He has a passion for golf and picked up the sport of curling several years ago. Michael recently achieved that perfect round of golf where he reached two under par. Michael is an avid gardener and landscaper. He has built several koi ponds and finds the sounds of the rushing water to be very relaxing and comforting.

Michael now lives in The Villages, Florida. As of 2024 he lives with his parents, where he helps take care of his 85-year old mother and 86-year old father.

One of Michael's new goals in life is to be able to help others through their life challenges by learning from his own experiences. As a business owner, divorced father, and a man who after fifty, discovered he lived most of his life fighting with a mental disorder. Michael wrote this book to hopefully help other people that might be getting ready or are currently going through a divorce, or possibly struggling with mental health issues, so that they are more prepared and equipped for life's "little" challenges.

Discover the
Power Within

Inside each one of us,
lies a wealth of untapped potential.
Don't let life's distractions
prevent you from
finding yours

Today is the start of the rest of your life,
embrace the adventure!

www.ingramcontent.com/pod-product-compliance
Lightning Source LLC
Chambersburg PA
CBHW030005290326
41934CB00005B/228